DIALECTICAL BEHAVIOR THERAPY
WORKBOOK

The 4 DBT Skills to Overcome Anxiety by Learning How to Manage Your Emotions. A Practical Guide to Recovering from Borderline Personality Disorder

DAVID LAWSON PhD

Table of Contents

INTRODUCTION

DBT works as a continuous relationship between clients and therapists. In this type of therapy, patients are encouraged to sort out their life problems in collaboration with their therapists. This demands that people role-play new methods of interacting with others, finish homework assignments, and rehearse skills like calming themselves when upset.

These skills form a crucial part of DBT and are taught to patients in weekly lectures and homework groups. In this way, individual therapists help their clients master the skills of DBT and apply them to their lives.

Four Stages of DBT

Treatment with DBT is commonly broken down into four levels. Clients are assigned to these levels based on the intensity of their behaviors. Therapists are instructed to follow the framework defined in these levels to help their clients. No specific timeframe has been allotted to these stages. The therapist and clients are allowed to take as much time as required, depending upon the client's target.

Level One

In level one, the patient is usually miserable and has lost control over themselves: they may be attempting to harm themselves, using drugs, or involving themselves in other self-destructive activities. When such clients start DBT, they may liken their experience to "being in hell."

The main goal of this stage is to help move the client from a state of no control to one in which they learn how to get a better hold of themselves.

Level Two

In level two, clients often feel like their lives are filled with desperation. They have control over their harmful behaviors, but they are still suffering, mostly due to invalidation or past trauma. This often continues to the extent that it disturbs their emotional experience.

The main goal of level two is to assist such people to get out of their state of desperation and to reinstate the emotional experience. The treatment for people suffering from post-traumatic stress disorder (PTSD) falls into this level.

Level Three

In this level, the aim is to motivate the patients to live, find happiness and peace, and build self-respect. The therapist enables the client to live a normal life with moments of both happiness and sadness.

Level Four

For some clients, an additional fourth level is required to familiarize them with the concept of spiritual existence. This stage has been created for clients whose life of happiness and sadness does not help them find peace or feel connected to the world.

The main goal of this stage is to assist the client in moving on from a feeling of incompleteness to a life which grants them the ability to enjoy the feeling of freedom and joy.

What Makes DBT Different?

The world is convinced that DBT can do wonders, but why is it that it continues to work even when gold-standard treatments like CBT have failed?

In simple words, DBT tends to fill in the gaps left behind by most other therapies, including CBT. For example, CBT emphasizes changing behaviors and thoughts to the extent that the clients can be appalled. Most therapies targeting problems like stress, anxiety, PTSD, etc. do not encourage or support their clients to accept where they are right now. They invalidate people by using cognitive distortions as justification that their feelings are wrong. That's where DBT differs.

DBT Promotes Acceptance-Based Behaviors

Dialectical Behavior Therapy is a form of CBT, but what makes it more successful and unique is its emphasis on dialectical thinking and mindfulness. Instead of treating the symptoms as problems to be solved, this therapy puts equal focus on the acceptance of experiences by incorporating acceptance-based behaviors.

Dialectical thinking is a philosophical stance in which two truths or ideas, which seemingly oppose each other, exist at the same time. For example, a person coming for help may need to accept where they are right now as well as requiring motivation to change.

In simpler words, while DBT helps people promote feelings of acceptance, it makes them acknowledge that they have the capacity to create more positivity and do much better. This is something that can exclusively be achieved through DBT.

DBT Works with Emotions

DBT is a form of in-depth therapy that involves the process of learning cognitive and emotional skills and applying these skills to your life. It helps tackle distressing and difficult emotions and helps you improve your capacity for emotional regulation. By improving your emotional regulation, you are able to control and express your emotions in a much better way.

DBT Enhances Capabilities with Skills Training

What makes DBT different to other approaches is that it focuses on improving the capabilities of clients by teaching them different behavioral skills. Skills training is taught in a classroom setup. A group leader is assigned to every class, and their primary responsibility is to teach different skills through classroom activities, lectures, and take-home assignments.

This homework helps the client apply the skills they learn in class to their daily experiences. The groups meet every week for about 2.5 hours to discuss the happenings in their daily lives. To grasp the full curriculum, an average person requires 24 weeks. Sometimes, the program may be repeated to form a 1-year program.

Skills Training in DBT revolves around four different modules, each of which helps the client become stable in their lives. These modules include:

Mindfulness: This is the skill which helps you become aware and present in the current moment.

Distress Tolerance: This refers to the skill which helps you tolerate pain in tough conditions, instead of changing the situation.

Interpersonal Effectiveness: This refers to the skill of asking for whatever you need and learning to say no without compromising your self-respect and in your relationships.

Emotional Regulation: This refers to the skill of changing the emotions you wish to change.

But how does acquiring these skills help people?

Problematic behaviors occur as a way to manage a situation or resolve a difficult problem. While such behaviors provide a temporary solution or relief in the short term, they are rarely effective in the long run. DBT acknowledges this and assumes that patients are doing everything in their capacity, but at the same time, they need to acquire new behavioral patterns in relevant contexts.

DBT helps such clients develop behavioral skills in the following four areas: emotional regulation, distress tolerance, mindfulness, and interpersonal effectiveness. These skills help clients acquire useful ways to navigate situations occurring in everyday life, and help them tackle challenges.

DBT Enhances Motivation Through Individual Therapy

DBT is an individual form of therapy that is focused on improving the client's motivation and helping them apply learned skills to tackle specific events in their lives. It is a unique approach that helps them accept their flaws, yet motivates them to get up and do better instead of treating them like victims who need sympathy.

DBT Ensures Generalization

DBT includes telephone coaching and other types of coaching to provide clients with in-the-moment support. The goal is to coach them on how to use DBT skills to cope with hard situations as they arise.

Therapists are available all the time to guide clients through difficult situations, which is something that seldom occurs in other therapy sessions.

DBT Structures the Environment via Case Management

DBT incorporates case management strategies that help the client manage their own life, including their social and physical environments. Therapists apply the same validation, problem-solving, and dialectical strategies to enable the client to analyze their problems without any external help. This empowers them to manage their problems on their own with minimal interference from a therapist unless absolutely necessary.

Thanks for downloading this book. It's my firm belief that it will provide you with all the answers to your questions.

CHAPTER 1: WHAT IS DIALECTICAL BEHAVIOR THERAPY?

Dialectical Behavior Therapy, or DBT, is a form of Cognitive Behavioral Therapy that focuses on solving behavioral problems by incorporating dialectical processes and acceptance-based strategies. It is best suited to the needs of patients suffering from intense emotional distress that prevents them from experiencing a good quality of life.

DBT was developed by American psychology researcher and author, Marsha Linehan. She created the therapy as a result of her struggles with schizophrenia and suicidal thoughts at a young age. She was institutionalized for her mental illness until the age of 18.

Convinced that CBT left a gap that needed to be filled, Linehan developed DBT at the University of Washington years later. DBT consists of four key skill areas and main components: interpersonal skills training, distress tolerance, emotional regulation, and mindfulness training.

DBT treatment can be delivered in many ways, typically consisting of individual therapy sessions and/or DBT skills groups. For example, while some patients may complete individual therapy sessions without attending any skills group, others might opt for group sessions without individual therapy.

An individual therapy session consists of a one-on-one session with a DBT therapist. This ensures that the patient's therapeutic needs are attended to. Over the course of the treatment, the therapist will also help the patient apply DBT skills on a daily basis, appropriately address daily struggles that occur, and stay motivated.

DBT skills groups, on the other hand, encourage members to learn and practice skills with each other while they are led by a DBT therapist. Members provide mutual support and listen as others share their experiences.

Therapists in a group session teach skills and lead members in group exercises. Each member is assigned homework, which often involves practicing mindfulness exercises.

Group sessions are typically completed within six months. Weekly sessions are conducted with each one lasting around two hours. The exact length of each session depends on the needs of each member.

HOW DBT WORKS

To build a life worth living, which is the main goal of DBT, client and therapist first sit down and make plans. They then set their goals and expectations.

There are five components in a standard DBT treatment program: a) a skills group, b) individual therapy, c) skills coaching, d) case management, and e) a consultation team. This section will provide an overview of the standard program.

Led by a therapist group leader, group sessions for teaching and learning behavioral skills happen every week and last about 2.5 hours. They are run like a class, and homework assignments are given so that patients can practice their newfound skills.

Twenty-four weeks are required for the entire skills curriculum, and this can be repeated to create a 1-year program. Depending on the situation and the needs of the patients, a shorter subset of this curriculum can also be taught.

The Four Skills Modules in DBT

The purpose of this skills group training is to improve clients' capabilities so they can effectively deal with the problems and challenges that arise in their daily lives. They learn from these four skills modules:

1. Mindfulness (being aware of ourselves and the situation we're in),
2. Distress tolerance (learning how to tolerate our pain in tough situations),
3. Interpersonal effectiveness (learning both assertiveness and respect of other people), and
4. Emotion regulation (learning how to change our negative emotions).

Of these four skills modules, mindfulness and distress tolerance belong to the acceptance strategy of DBT; interpersonal effectiveness and emotion regulation belong to the change strategy.

Individual Therapy

The purpose of an individual psychotherapy session is to improve the motivation of each patient. Personal issues and struggles are talked about, with the therapist encouraging the patient in the light of DBT's focus on acceptance and change. Skills learned in group sessions are also reinforced. Furthermore, a real relationship of mutual help between therapist and patient is formed; the therapist becomes a true partner in the process, not just a teacher or observer.

Like with the skills group training, an individual therapy session happens every week and runs concurrently with it.

Skills Coaching

DBT patients can call their therapists at any time of the day, to ask for advice whenever problems arise. The goal of skills coaching is to train patients to practice and apply the skills they are learning in their lives.

Case Management

This is about helping patients manage their own lives. The therapist advises on the things to be done but intervenes only when necessary.

The Consultation Team

The therapists themselves are part of a consultation team, in which they are given support for the work they are doing. This way, they will stay motivated and competent. This kind of emotional support is especially needed for difficult cases.

Clients who choose to undergo Dialectical Behavior Therapy often have several behavioral problems to be treated, not just one. The therapist will then have to prioritize problems according to the following hierarchy: (1) threat to life, (2) interference to therapy, (3) interference to quality of life, and (4) the need to learn new skills. For example, suicidal thoughts of a patient will be dealt with first, before alcohol abuse.

Lastly, there are 3 to 4 stages of treatment for DBT. Stage 1 corresponds to the initial life of the patient being out of control. Stage 2 corresponds to continued silent suffering after some control has already been achieved. Stage 3 corresponds to the challenge of living life: setting goals, gaining self-respect, finding happiness. And Stage 4, which is needed only by some, corresponds to finding a deeper fulfillment and completeness through spirituality of some kind.

IS DIALECTICAL BEHAVIOR THERAPY REALLY EFFECTIVE?

So, does it really work? The answer is a resounding yes. DBT is a treatment based on evidence, and research has shown that it is indeed effective against the mental health illnesses it is used on, which are many. It is also found to be effective on people of diverse backgrounds (in terms of age, gender, sexual orientation, and race), and it's already been implemented in more than 25 countries.

DBT has also received recognition from official authorities, like the American Psychological Association.

CHAPTER 2: DBT APPLICATIONS

DBT is most effective for people who experience emotions very intensely. They tend to be easily overwhelmed by life and relational stressors to the point that they feel that their emotional responses are out of control. Consequently, they often act in an impulsive manner in an attempt to temporarily relieve some of their distress. However, their reactions over the long term tend to create additional problems.

DBT was initially used to help individuals who were diagnosed with Borderline Personality Disorder (BPD). This was and continues to be a very effective form of therapy to use with these individuals. However, in more recent years, DBT has also been very successfully used with other individuals who demonstrate severe mood swings and are unable to apply coping strategies to successfully deal with these intense and sudden emotional urges. Many of these people struggle with severe depression, PTSD, eating disorders, severe compulsory disorders, Bipolar Disorder, ADHD, anger management, and/or substance abuse. Many people who seek out DBT also engage in self-harm, as this therapy has been shown to be very effective in helping individuals with this level of emotional trouble.

In order to really understand more about the person who generally does well in DBT, let's take a look at the specific characteristics that many of these people share. People who do well with DBT usually have a high level of emotional vulnerability. What this means is that they are prone to experiencing emotions in a very reactive and intense way. Sometimes, they are just hardwired to feel emotions more intensely than the average person. In fact, DBT theory asserts that the automatic nervous system of an emotionally vulnerable person is predisposed to be reactive to relatively low levels of stress. Their nervous system also takes much longer to return to baseline levels when the stressor is removed. Additionally, some people have mood disorders such as major depression or generalized anxiety that is not being effectively controlled by medication, and that influence how intensely they experience their emotions. Consequently, emotionally vulnerable people tend to have quick, intense, emotional reactions that are difficult to control. This keeps them on a roller coaster ride throughout their lives.

However, clinicians have found that most emotionally vulnerable people who seek DBT treatment are not JUST hardwired to have more intense emotions or have mood disorders. Typically, they have also been exposed to invalidating environments for extensive periods of time. Such environments generally stem from early childhood, but could have occurred at any point. These environments did not provide them with the support, attention, respect, or understanding that they needed to properly work through their emotions. Invalidating environments can range from ones involving severe emotional or physical abuse to mismatched parent and child personalities. Consider the shy child who is born or adopted into a family full of extroverts, and who is constantly teased about his or her introverted personality. Or perhaps it's the child with ADHD who has a mother and stepfather who are inflexible and constantly yelling at them. These are both examples of environments that are invalidating. When the person who already has a predisposition to experience more extreme emotions is placed in an environment that does not support or validate their feelings, they can become even more emotionally vulnerable. They may then begin to demonstrate even greater emotional reactivity because they inadvertently learned that the only time they were taken seriously was when they demonstrated extremely emotional behavior.

Let's take the introverted child as an example, and let's say it's a boy. Say he was constantly told by his father that he had to "man up" and become more aggressive in his approach to life. He felt ridiculed and began to think that there was something wrong with him. So, one day when his father was addressing him, the boy began to cry uncontrollably. His father immediately lightened up, and his mother came rushing to his aid, showering him with tons of attention. Then it happened again. And then again. An interesting thing began to happen. The young boy's unconscious mind began to see a pattern that looked like this: 'My dad harasses me, I cry uncontrollably, the hassling stops, I get lots of attention.' He began to do it more and more because it worked and each successful demonstration inadvertently reinforced the behavior. His emotional outbursts became validated, and then it ultimately becomes an ingrained coping skill.

The process described above unconsciously reinforced the child's emotional vulnerability, and you guessed it – made it worse. This is typically the pattern you see with people with Borderline Personality Disorder, Bipolar Disorder, eating disorders, and other disorders that DBT treats. The next section will give an overview of several of the disorders that are successfully treated with DBT.

Borderline Personality Disorder

People with Borderline Personality Disorder (BPD) experience emotions more intensely and for longer periods of time than other people. They are prone to frequent and chronic outbursts to the point that many mental health professionals have described this population as one that is experiencing an unrelenting crisis. They are nearly always in crisis mode as they have generally not learned the coping skills they need to better regulate their intense emotions.

Individuals with BPD are emotionally vulnerable, and it takes them much longer to return to baseline following an event. In addition, one of the patterns that therapists have described regarding people with BPD is their tendency to take on the same belief system as the invalidating environment that they are subjected to. This results in their own "self-invalidation," where they reject their own emotions and ability to solve problems. They also tend to develop unrealistic expectations for themselves and experience intense shame and anger when they fail to meet their goals or when difficulties arise.

Another defining characteristic of individuals with BPD is their tendency to make rigid and unrealistic demands of themselves and others. When things don't go as they planned or desire, they often resort to "blaming." Blaming is a thinking error that many people with BPD have. They blame everyone and everything for their problems and have trouble acknowledging the personal behavioral changes that need to be made in order to see different outcomes in their lifestyle.

Individuals with BPD have a poor sense of self and tend to struggle with interpersonal relationships. They tend to seek out individuals who will take control and solve their problems for them so that they can shrink back and not have to do so. However, they tend to wear the mask of competence so that others think that they are capable of solving their own problems and dealing with their intense emotions. Although they may have mastered certain areas of their life, they have not been successful at generalizing their competence in other areas.

Due to the lifestyle that most people with BDP have created, in combination with their difficulties in returning to baseline following an emotional event, they end up experiencing significant traumatic experiences on an ongoing basis. They also tend to avoid experiencing negative emotions altogether because they do not know how to regulate even healthy negative emotions. As a result, they do not know what to do when an emotional situation arises that they are unable to tolerate, which throws them into an intense and prolonged emotional state.

People with Borderline Personality Disorder sometimes engage in cutting or other self-harm and suicidal behavior to deal with the intense emotional pain. Emotional vulnerability is often seen in individuals who are suicidal or engage in chronic self-injury. The individual is highly emotionally reactive, and when exposed to very severe trauma such as physical or emotional abuse, they begin to think about suicide. Eventually, in an attempt to be relieved of the ongoing pain, they try to kill themselves and are taken to hospital. Here, they are given loads of attention, and for the first time, they begin to feel like they are being validated and taken seriously.

Consider the boy who engages in some type of self-injury, such as cutting or burning himself because he finds that it provides temporary relief. When someone else finds out that this is happening, people are suddenly taking him seriously. Similar to the experience of the first example, he is finally feeling validated.

What do you think happens in these two situations? Over time, the boys both continue to engage in these behaviors, because it is the only time they feel validated and supported. It becomes an ingrained coping skill.

Eating Disorders

An eating disorder is an illness whereby a person has eating habits that are considered irregular. However, the illness goes beyond simple disruption of food intake, as the person experiencing the eating disorder generally feels severe distress regarding their body weight and/or shape. In an attempt to regulate their appearance and feel better about themselves, people with eating disorders may begin to eat significantly less and become obsessed with exercise. This emotional and behavioral disturbance can occur in both sexes and generally has an extreme impact on the physical and emotional well-being of the person.

Although eating disorders can occur at any developmental stage, they typically emerge during adolescence or early adulthood and often coexist with other psychological and behavioral conditions such as substance abuse, mood disorders, and anxiety disorders. The three most common types of eating disorders are discussed below.

Anorexia Nervosa

An individual who experiences anorexia nervosa usually demonstrates a strong obsession with their weight. Due to their poor and unrealistic perceptions of body image, they are fearful of gaining weight and often refuse to maintain a weight that is healthy. Many people who struggle with this disorder limit the amount of food they eat to the point that their caloric intake cannot sustain their health. Even when they are visibly underweight and their appearance begins to generate concern in others, they continue to view themselves as overweight. Anorexia can lead to major health issues such as infertility, heart problems, organ failure, brain damage, and bone loss. People with this disease have a high risk of death.

Bulimia Nervosa

Individuals who struggle with bulimia generally fear being overweight and are very unhappy with the appearance of their body. This disorder is characterized by the cycle of binge eating followed by overcompensation for the binge eating. For example, a person may sit and eat excessive amounts of food in one sitting and then follow the eating with forced vomiting, excessive exercise, extreme use of laxatives and diuretics, or any combination of these compensatory behaviors. The cycle is done in secret as they generally harbor a lot of shame, guilt, and lack of self-control. Bulimia can also lead to health problems such as gastrointestinal problems, dehydration, and heart issues that result from an imbalance of electrolytes caused by the eating-purging cycle.

Binge Eating Disorder

Individuals who struggle with binge eating often lose control of their eating but do not engage in the purging process as with bulimia. Consequently, many people who experience binge eating may also have the corresponding disorder of obesity, which increases health-related problems such as heart disease. As with individuals with other eating disorders, individuals who battle this disorder often have feelings of intense shame, guilt, embarrassment, and feelings of loss of control.

It is believed that the development of eating disorders is multifaceted, as the disorders are generally quite complex. Some of the things that contribute to the emergence of an eating disorder include biological, psychological, and of course, environmental factors. These factors include:

- Biological factors such as irregular hormone functions and a genetic predisposition
- Nutritional deficiencies
- Psychological factors such as a negative body image and poor self-esteem
- Environmental factors such as a dysfunctional family unit
- Professions and careers that promote excessive thinness – like modeling
- Sports that promote thinness for performance such as gymnastics, wrestling, long-distance running, and others
- Sexual abuse in childhood
- Family, peer, and media pressure to be thin
- Transitions and life changes

Here are some of the signs and symptoms that someone may exhibit when struggling with an eating disorder:

- Chronic and excessive dieting even when underweight
- Obsession with caloric intake and the fat content of food
- Demonstrating eating patterns that are ritualistic. These rituals might include behaviors like eating alone, breaking food into small pieces, and hiding food for later consumption
- A fixation on food. Some individuals with eating disorders may prepare delicious complex meals for other people but refuse to eat the meal.
- People with eating disorders may also suffer from depression or lethargy

Although DBT has been shown to be very successful in treating individuals with eating disorders, they may need additional support in the early stages of treatment. Additional support may include being monitored by a physician to address any health issues that may have developed as well as working with a nutritionist until weight is stabilized. Often, the nutritionist will develop an individualized meal plan to help individuals return to a healthy weight.

Bipolar Disorder

This is also often referred to as Manic Depressive Disorder because of the individual's tendency to vacillate between manic episodes and more depressive states. This disorder is characterized by unusual and extreme changes in activity levels, energy levels, mood, and the ability to perform daily tasks. The symptoms are not the same as normal mood fluctuations, as they are severe and generally quite extreme to the point that individuals may damage relationships, jeopardize performance at work and school, and even contemplate suicide.

Like most psychological disorders, there is generally no single cause for Bipolar Disorder. It is often an illness that develops from a combination of biological and environmental factors. Many factors act together to produce the illness or increase the risk of the illness manifesting.

Genetics seems to play a role in the emergence of Bipolar Disorder as research has identified some genes that are more likely to influence the development of the disorder. Other research has shown that children from particular families or those who have a sibling with the disorder are more likely to develop the disorder themselves.

However, research has also shown that environmental factors play a strong role in its emergence. In identical twin studies where siblings share the same exact genetic makeup, when one twin develops the disorder, the other twin does not always. This indicates that something other than genetics is at work, which points to environmental triggers.

Individuals with this condition experience strong emotional states known as "mood episodes." Each episode can last for days or months. Each episode reflects an extreme change in presentation from the person's normal behavior. An exceedingly joyful, ecstatic state that is full of increased activity is typically the "manic" episode. The sad, dysphoric, hopeless, and sometimes irritable and explosive state is the "depressive" episode. A "mixed state" is when behavior characteristics of both a manic and depressive episode are present at the same time.

Here are some symptoms that are characteristic of Bipolar Disorder:

The manic episode includes symptoms such as:

- Feeling "high" for a long period, demonstrated by an excessively happy mood
- Fast-talking and hopping from one idea to another. This is reflective of running thoughts.
- Being easily distracted
- Excessive activity level and taking on many new projects
- Restlessness
- Limited sleep
- Unrealistic thoughts about what one can do
- Impulsiveness and preoccupation with pleasurable and risky activities

The characteristics of a depressive episode include:

- Long periods of extreme irritability
- Long periods of sadness or hopelessness
- Losing interest in events that a person once loved
- Tiredness and feeling sluggish
- Difficulties remembering, concentrating, and decision making
- Change in eating, sleeping, and other habits
- Suicidal ideation, gestures, and/or suicidal attempts may also be present

Bipolar Disorder can occur even when a person's mood swings are low. For example, hypomania, which is not severe, is experienced by some individuals with Bipolar Disorder. The individual may feel good during a hypomanic episode and is even highly productive. However, though they are functioning well, their friends and family note the significant difference in mood. The mood change is so remarkable that family and friends may wonder if symptoms of Bipolar Disorder are present. Hypomania may easily become full mania or symptoms of Bipolar Disorder may occur if a person does not get proper treatment.

As previously mentioned, Bipolar Disorder can be present in a mixed state. This is when a person experiences both depression and mania simultaneously. In a mixed state, one may feel very disturbed, experience sleep disruption, lose their appetite, and may even think of committing suicide. Individuals in this state may have a feeling of being hopeless or sad while still feeling extremely energized.

When experiencing a severe episode of depression or mania, an individual can experience psychotic symptoms such as delusions or hallucinations, as well. The psychotic signs tend to show and strengthen the extreme mood of an individual. For instance, if a person has psychotic signs in a manic episode, he may believe that he is the president of a country, has vast wealth, or has some kind of special power. Psychotic signs in a depressive episode might include believing that she is homeless, ruined, penniless, or a criminal on the run. Unfortunately, sometimes individuals with this condition are misdiagnosed with schizophrenia or another reality testing disorder because of their mood-induced hallucinations.

Individuals with Bipolar Disorder also often have the co-occurring disorder of polysubstance abuse or dependence. Anxiety disorders, such as Post-Traumatic Stress Disorder (PTSD) and phobias, also co-occur quite often. Bipolar Disorder also sometimes co-occurs with Attention Deficit Hyperactivity Disorder (ADHD). People with Bipolar Disorder also have a higher likelihood of diabetes, headaches, thyroid disease, heart disease, migraine obesity, and other physical sicknesses.

Bipolar Disorder usually begins to develop in the late teenage years or during early adulthood. However, some people have their first symptoms during childhood, while others may develop symptoms later on in life. At least half of all cases start before the age of 25.

Types of Bipolar Disorder are as follows:

- Bipolar I Disorder
- Bipolar II Disorder
- Bipolar Disorder Not Otherwise Specified (BP-NOS)
- Cyclothymic Disorder or Cyclothymia

If not diagnosed and treated, the bipolar condition can become worse. It becomes severe as episodes become frequent. This delay can result in the person demonstrating behavior that significantly impacts relationships, personal goals, finances, housing, work, school, and many other areas. DBT has been known to help individuals with this condition lead healthier and more productive lives. Many times, DBT has helped individuals decrease the episodes' severity and frequency.

Post-Traumatic Stress Disorder (PTSD)

The body has a built-in and naturally occurring mechanism that makes individuals seek to escape danger. This mechanism is known as the fight-or-flight response. When your brain receives the signal that there is imminent danger, your body goes into an automatic response mode. You naturally begin to feel afraid and your body gears up to either flee the situation to get to safety or to fight to ensure your self-preservation and survival. Your fear of dangerous situations triggers many split-second and unconscious changes in the body that prepares you to either flee or fight in a particular situation. This is a natural process that is biologically incorporated to help people protect themselves from harm. However, in certain individuals, repeated exposure to trauma, or exposure to one extremely high-level traumatic experience causes this normal "fight-or-flight" response to go haywire. When this process is damaged, and individuals become stressed or frightened even when they are no longer in danger, this is called Post-Traumatic Stress Disorder (PTSD).

PTSD generally occurs after someone experiences a terrifying and/or life-threatening ordeal. The ordeal usually involves some type of actual physical harm or threat of physical harm. The harm or threat to harm may have involved the person themselves, a loved one, or the person may have witnessed a harmful event that happened to someone else or a group of other people. Some examples of situations that can cause PTSD are:

- War
- Rape or sexual abuse
- Terrorism
- Robbery
- Train wrecks
- Car accidents
- Plane crashes
- Natural disasters such as floods, earthquakes, and tornadoes
- Childhood physical abuse
- Domestic violence
- Hostage situations
- Torture
- Bombings
- Any other very traumatic event

PTSD is caused by a combination of genetic and environmental features. The way that a specific individual is biologically wired to deal with fear sensations and memories has a lot to do with the development of PTSD. People who are more emotionally vulnerable to fear due to their brain chemistry are more likely to develop PTSD.

Environmental factors also play a significant role in the emergence of PTSD. Environmental factors such as trauma that occurred in childhood, head injuries, or a personal history of mental illness may also increase a person's risk of developing the disorder. Also, personality and cognitive factors such as thinking errors, ability to tolerate distress, pessimism, and other cognitive-related factors increase risk. Similarly, social factors such as the availability of a support system help people adjust to trauma and may help them avoid the experience of PTSD.

PTSD Symptoms

PTSD symptoms are categorized into three groups:

1. Re-experiencing symptoms

- Flashbacks.

- Nightmares about the event.

- Frightening thoughts that are intrusive and persistent. They pop up out of seemingly nowhere, and they are hard to get rid of.

Obviously, re-experiencing symptoms can be very disruptive to day to day functioning. They may cause problems in a person's everyday routine and interpersonal relationships.

2. Avoidance symptoms

- These symptoms are demonstrated when a person avoids anything that reminds them of the traumatic incident. They stay away because going near them triggers an out of control emotional response.

- Feeling emotionally numb is also an avoidant type of symptom. Rather than risk feeling an intense negative emotion, they feel emotionally numb. They avoid any emotional experience at all in an attempt to avoid negative feelings.

- Victims feeling strong worry, depression, or guilt without really knowing why is another example of an avoidant symptom. Rather than deal with the response to the incident directly, people with PTSD may have more generalized negative feelings.

- Victims may experience a loss of interest in activities they previously loved. Avoidance of all pleasurable activity is characteristic of PTSD.

- Difficulties in remembering the dangerous incident are also common. Rather than deal with what happened, sometimes it's easier to just stuff the whole experience into the subconscious. This is an example of avoidance.

- Change in routine is also avoidant in nature. Sometimes, people with PTSD will purposefully change their routines so they don't have to worry about dealing with a trigger. An example of this would be if a person avoids driving a car after a life-threatening car accident. This was very common after 9-11 when many people refused to get on airplanes after the terrorist attack.

3. Hyperarousal symptoms

- People recovering from PTSD are often easily startled, and they may feel tense more frequently than before the traumatic event.

- Their automatic nervous system is more active, so they experience troubles in sleeping and managing their anger. Angry outbursts may occur frequently.

- It should be noted that hyperarousal symptoms are usually constant and are present even without a specific trigger.

- It's completely natural for someone to experience one or even several of these symptoms after being involved in an event that is traumatic.

Keep in mind that children and teenagers may present differently when they are experiencing PTSD. In young kids, you may see:

- Reverting back to bedwetting after they have been potty trained
- Not talking after reaching a verbal developmental stage
- Reenactment of the traumatizing event when playing

In older children or adolescents, you may see symptoms that are more consistent with adult symptoms. However, you may also see an increase in disrespectful and explosive behavior. They can also become preoccupied with getting revenge or feel guilty for not doing more to prevent the event or the injuries that occurred in response to the event.

PTSD can happen at any age. Females have a higher risk of developing PTSD, and there seems to be a significant genetic link. Not all people who live through a risky event develop this condition.

There are several factors that determine if an individual will develop PTSD. Factors that increase the probability an individual getting PTSD are called risk factors. Factors that lower a person's chances of getting PTSD are called resilience factors. Some of these risk and resilience factors are present before the trauma, while others develop during or after a traumatic event.

Resilience factors for PTSD include:

- Access to an adequate support system following a trauma
- Having an effective coping strategy
- Feeling good about individual actions when there's trouble

- Therapy or counseling that addresses adjustment post-trauma

Risk factors for PTSD include:

- Experiencing a trauma
- Personal history of mental illness
- Physical injury
- Witnessing people getting killed or hurt
- Inadequate or lack of social support after an incident
- Loss of a home, job or a loved one

Obsessive Compulsive Disorder (OCD)

This is a psychological disorder that has the potential to be quite disabling if left untreated. It traps people into a relentless and never-ending series of behaviors and thoughts that are repetitive. They become overwhelmed with thoughts, fears, and images that they cannot control. So, they instead obsess about them continuously. These endless and negative thoughts produce anxiety that causes these individuals to feel an urgent and immediate need to engage in certain rituals, routines, or safety-seeking behavior. These compulsive behaviors are the person's way of trying to eliminate the anxiety that comes with obsessive and ruminating thoughts.

Although the ritualistic behavior generally does temporarily alleviate the anxiety, it becomes a chronic problem because the person must carry out the ritual again when the obsessive thoughts come back. This OCD cycle can really begin to impact the person's relationships and even personal health. It is not uncommon for a person with OCD to take up hours of their time that they would normally be using to engage in normal activities to complete the ritualistic tasks. People with OCD are often aware of their behavior, and they know that their rituals are unrealistic and problematic, but they cannot stop them.

Common obsessions include:

- Fear of dirt
- Fear of causing harm to others
- Fear of making a mistake
- Fear of being embarrassed
- Fear of behaving in a socially unacceptable manner
- Fear of thinking thoughts that are sinful or evil
- Excessive doubt and the need for constant reassurance

Common compulsions include:

- Repeating specific prayers, phrases, or words
- Washing hands, showering or bathing repeatedly
- Eating in a certain order
- Having to do errands a certain number of times
- Declining to touch doorknobs or shake hands
- Hoarding

While it is not entirely known what causes OCD, research has indicated that a mixture of environmental and biological factors is involved, consistent with most other mental and behavioral health disorders.

Biological Factors

It is thought by researchers that OCD comes from problems in the pathways that link the parts of the brain that deal with planning and judgment with the part responsible for filtering body movement messages. Moreover, some evidence shows that OCD is passed to children from their parents.

Environmental Factors

Environmental stressors can cause OCD in some individuals. Other factors may make the symptoms worse. Some of these are:

- Abuse
- Moving house
- Sickness
- Work changes
- Death of someone close
- School problems
- Relationship concerns

A recent statistic indicated that 1 million children and adolescents, and 3.3 million adults, are affected by OCD in the United States. This disorder responds well to therapies such as CBT and DBT.

Severe Major Depression

Almost everyone has experienced some level of sadness in their life. Sadness is a normal emotional response to bad situations. However, when sadness becomes so pronounced that it interferes with daily performance and activities, help may be needed.

Major depression or clinical depression is characterized by a depressed mood that is prevalent throughout the day and can be particularly prevalent in the morning. The disorder is characterized by a lack of interest in relationships and normal chores and symptoms are present every day for at least 2 weeks.

Here are the typical symptoms of major depression:

- Fatigue
- Indecisiveness
- Feeling guilty
- Reduced concentration
- Insomnia or hypersomnia
- Sluggishness or restlessness
- Recurring thoughts of death or suicide
- Weight gain or loss

Major depression affects almost 10% of the US population over the age of 18. Some statistics indicate that between 20% and 25% of all US adults suffer an episode of major depression at some point during their lifetime. Major depression also affects elderly adults, teenagers, and children, but unfortunately, the disorder often goes undiagnosed and untreated in these populations.

Almost twice as many women as men have been diagnosed with major or clinical depression, which means that more women than men will likely be in treatment. Hormonal changes, pregnancy, miscarriage, and menopause may also increase the risk. Other factors that boost the risk of clinical depression in women who are biologically vulnerable include environmental stressors such as increased stress at home or work, balancing family life with career, and caring for an aging parent. Being a single parent has also been shown to increase the risk of depression.

It is believed that one of the reasons that women outnumber men diagnosed with major depression is because men are less likely to report symptoms. In fact, major depression in men is extremely underreported. Unfortunately, men who suffer from clinical depression are less likely to seek help or even talk about their experience.

Signs of depression in men may be a little different than in women. Here's what you can expect to see:

- Increased irritability and anger
- Substance abuse
- Violent behavior directed both inwardly and outwardly (due to repressed feelings)
- Reckless behavior
- Deterioration of health
- Increase risk of suicide and homicide

Here are triggers that are common:

- Grief from losing a loved one through separation, divorce, or death
- Major life changes such as moving, graduating, job change, promotion, retirement, and having children
- Being isolated socially
- Relationship conflict with a partner or supervisor
- Divorce
- Emotional, sexual, or physical abuse

Individuals who experience the various disorders described in this section experience extreme difficulty regulating their emotions. In addition, there is generally a social component that contributes to the manifestation of the disorder. DBT takes the psychosocial components that traditional CBT therapies take into consideration with the intention of helping individuals learn how to manage their out-of-control emotions and behaviors. As you will see in the following chapters, two of the models of DBT emphasize acceptance while two of them emphasize change so that the individual feels both validated and motivated to make the necessary behavioral changes.

CHAPTER 3: WHY MINDFULNESS IS
A SUPERPOWER

Mindfulness is having a wise mind and being present in the moment. There are many facets to being mindful. It consists of observing, describing, and participating in the present moment. What does it mean to do these things? It means not to let your mind wander. Bring it back to the present moment.

Even if you don't have BPD, or any diagnosed mental illness, learning mindfulness and learning how to live in the present without worrying about the future or the past is a useful skill for anyone.

Mindfulness is a basic psychotherapy technique used to treat anxiety, anger, depression, and other psychological problems. While it has its roots in the mysticism of eastern cultures, western science has studied the subject a great deal. Psychotherapists even recommend mindfulness meditation for individuals who are suffering from certain mental health problems. Developing mindfulness is a crucial part of CBT, as well as DBT and ACT (Acceptance and Commitment Therapy). In fact, it is one of the four skills modules in DBT.

Basically, mindfulness is the state of mind that can be achieved by focusing our awareness on what is happening in the present. It also involves the calm acceptance of our feelings, sensations, and thoughts.

The challenge of focusing on the present may seem trivial for some, but this is actually easier said than done. Our mind may wander away, we lose touch with the present moment, and we may even be absorbed into obsessive thoughts about the things that have happened in the past or worry about the future. But regardless of how far our mind drifts from the present, we can use mindfulness to immediately get us back to what we are presently doing or feeling.

Even though it is natural for us to be mindful anytime we want, we can further cultivate mindfulness through effective ACT techniques that you will learn later on.

Mindfulness is usually linked with meditation. While meditation is an effective way to achieve mindfulness, there's more to it. Mindfulness is a form of being present, which you can use any time. It is a form of consciousness that you can achieve if you intentionally focus on the present moment without any judgment.

ELEMENTS OF MINDFULNESS

Attention and attitude are the two primary elements of mindfulness.

Attention

Many of us suffer from what is known as "monkey mind," whereby the mind behaves like a monkey swinging from one branch to another. Our mind may swing away and back again, and we usually don't have any idea how we ended up thinking about something.

The monkey mind usually dwells in the past, ruminating on what has happened or what you think would have happened if you had acted differently. It also swings away to the future, being anxious about what could happen. Nourishing the monkey mind will steal away the experience of the present moment.

Remember, mindfulness is focusing your attention on what is happening now.

Attitude

Suspending judgment and kindness are the basic tenets of mindfulness. Hence, a genuinely mindful person knows how to accept reality and doesn't engage in arguing with it. This may seem an easy task, but once you begin practicing mindfulness, you will become aware of how frequently we judge ourselves and our thoughts.

Here are some examples of sentences used in the judgment of ourselves and others:

- I'm not good at this task.
- My shirt looks lame.
- I don't like my home.
- I really don't like my neighbor.
- What a grumpy waitress.

Mindfulness is also the art of calming our inner judge. It allows us to erase our internal expectations and become more embracing of how things are in the present moment. But take note that this doesn't mean you don't need to make necessary changes.

Remember, you are only suspending your judgment so you can have more time to think about the situation and do something about it. The main difference is that you can make changes from an ideal state of mind for change and not during times that you are influenced by tension or stress.

Moreover, mindfulness will allow you to be more compassionate with yourself, more embracing of your experience, and more caring of the people around you. It will also allow you to be more patient and non-judgmental if you have some lapses. As you practice mindfulness, you can reshape your brain to become kinder and more compassionate.

HOW MINDFULNESS CAN RESHAPE YOUR BRAIN

In the past, people believed that the human brain could only develop to a certain level, usually from early childhood to adolescence. But various studies have revealed that our brain has the capacity to reorganize itself through forming neural connections. This is known as neuroplasticity, and it has no virtually no limits.

Neuroscientists shattered the old belief that the human brain is an unchanging, static organ. They discovered that despite age, disease, or injury, the human brain can compensate for any damage by restructuring itself. To put it simply, our brain is capable of repairing itself.

Studies also support the idea that mindfulness can significantly help in the brain's development. It specifically helps in the process of neuroplasticity. It is really amazing to know that we can change our emotions, feelings, and thought processes through neuroplasticity and mindfulness.

There are three major studies that show how mindfulness can rewire the human brain through neuroplasticity.

Mindfulness Can Improve Memory, Learning, and Other Cognitive Functions

Even though mindfulness meditation is linked with a sense of physical relaxation and calmness, practitioners claim the practice can also help in learning and memory.

Sara Lazar, a professor at Harvard University Medical School, pioneered an 8-week meditation program that primarily uses mindfulness. With her team of researchers from Massachusetts General Hospital, she conducted the program to explore the connection between mindfulness and the improvement of cognitive functions.

The program was composed of weekly meditation sessions as well as audio recordings for the 16 volunteers who practiced meditation alone. On average, the participants practiced meditation for around 27 minutes. The underlying concept of mindfulness meditation for research was on achieving a state of mind in which the participants suspend their judgment and just focus on feeling sensations.

Later, the team used Magnetic Resonance Imaging (MRI) to capture images of the brain structure of the participants. A group of individuals who were not meditating (the control group) were also asked for an MRI scan.

The researchers were amazed by the result. Primarily, the study participants revealed that they experienced significant cognitive advantages that were proven in their responses in the mindfulness survey. On top of that, researchers also noted measurable physical differences in the density of the gray matter as supported by MRI scan.

- The gray-matter density in the amygdala, the area of the brain responsible for stress and anxiety, was decreased.
- There were significant changes in the brain areas responsible for self-awareness, introspection, and compassion.
- The gray-matter density in the hippocampus, the part of the brain responsible for memory and learning, was increased.

This Harvard study reveals that neuroplasticity, through practicing meditation, can play an active role in the development of our brain. It is exciting to know that we can do something every day to improve our quality of life and general well-being.

Mindfulness Can Help Combat Depression

Millions of people around the world suffer from depression. For example, in the US, there are about 19 million people who are seeking medication to combat depression. This is around 10% of the whole US population.

Dr. Zindel Segal, a Psychiatry Professor at the University of Toronto, used a research grant from the MacArthur Foundation to explore the advantages of mindfulness towards alleviating depression. The research, that was mainly focused on the administration of mindfulness-based stress reduction sessions, was considered a success, and he conducted follow-up research to study the effectiveness of mindfulness meditation in patients afflicted by depression. This has resulted in the establishment of Mindfulness-Based Cognitive Therapy or MBCT.

The study involved patients suffering from depression, with 8 out of 10 having experienced at least three episodes of depression. Following the stress reduction sessions, around 30% of participants who experienced at least three episodes of depression did not relapse for more than a year, in comparison to those who followed prescribed other therapies such as antidepressants.

Segal's study has become a precursor to studies sponsored by Oxford and Cambridge Universities in the United Kingdom, with both studies generating similar outcomes. The research has proved significantly valuable in using mindfulness meditation as an effective and healthier alternative to medication in the UK, and has convinced mental health practitioners to prescribe mindfulness meditation to their patients.

Mindfulness meditation and research studies on MBCT are gradually gaining a foothold within medical and scientific circles in the US and other parts of the globe.

Mindfulness Can Help in Stress Relief

A study conducted at Carnegie Mellon University has revealed that the practice of mindfulness, even for 25 minutes a day, can alleviate stress. The study, led by Prof. David Creswell, involved 66 participants aged between 18 and 30 years.

One group of study subjects was asked to undergo a short meditation session composed of 25 minutes of mindfulness for three days. This group was asked to do some exercises designed to get them to concentrate on their breathing while turning their focus to the present moment. The second group used the same time to assess poetry readings to improve their problem-solving skills.

During the evaluation phase, all the participants were asked to complete math and speech tasks in front of evaluators who were asked to look stern. All participants reported their stress levels increased and were asked for saliva samples to measure the levels of the stress hormone cortisol.

The group who was asked to practice mindfulness meditation for at least 25 minutes for three days reported less stress during the task, showing that practicing mindfulness even in the short term can increase the body's ability to handle stress.

It is interesting to note that the same group showed higher levels of the stress hormone, which was not expected by the researchers.

The research concluded that when participants learn mindfulness meditation, they have to actively work on the process – particularly in a stressful situation. The cognitive task may feel less stressful for the individual, despite an elevated cortisol level.

The team is now focusing on automating the mindfulness sessions to make it less stressful while reducing cortisol levels. But it is clear that even in the initial phases, short-term meditation can do a great deal in relieving stress.

OTHER BENEFITS OF MINDFULNESS

Aside from the benefits described above, mindfulness meditation provides great benefits for our emotional, mental, and physical health.

Emotional Benefits

Mindfulness allows us to be more compassionate. Those who practice mindfulness meditation show changes in specific areas of the brain that are associated with empathy.

Mindfulness meditation decreases our reactivity to our emotions. A study conducted in the Massachusetts General Hospital revealed that mindfulness reduces the size of the amygdala, which is responsible for fear, anxiety, and aggression.

Mindfulness meditation can help us avoid negative thoughts, which our brain usually resorts to once left on its own.

In 2007, a study was conducted among students who were taught meditation strategies. It revealed that mindfulness helped the students increase their focus and decrease self-doubt, anxiety, and depression. There was also a notable decrease in suspensions and absenteeism in schools where mindfulness sessions were encouraged.

Mindfulness is also now used to ease symptoms of anxiety and depression. Many psychotherapists now prescribe mindfulness meditation for patients who are suffering from depressive episodes.

Mental Health Benefits

A study published in the *Journal of Psychological Science* revealed that students who practiced meditation before taking an exam got better results compared to students who did not. The study discovered a link between mindfulness and better cognitive function.

Mindfulness increases the activity in the anterior cingulate, which is the part of the brain responsible for memory, learning, and emotional regulation. It also increases activity in the prefrontal cortex that is responsible for judgment and planning.

Mindfulness is linked to improved concentration and longer attention span.

Mindfulness meditation also increases the brain's neural connections and has been proven to fortify myelin, which is the protective tissue that surrounds the neurons responsible for transmitting signals in the brain.

Physical Benefits

Deep breathing can deactivate our sympathetic nervous system, which is responsible for our fight or flight response. It also activates the parasympathetic nervous system that is responsible for our rest and digest mode.

Mindfulness decreases the level of cortisol in the body. This stress hormone increases levels of stress and encourages hypertension.

In one study, participants who practiced mindfulness meditation reduced their risk of heart attack by more than five years and also reduced their blood pressure.

Mindfulness allows our mind to become aware of what we eat and has been used for weight loss programs.

Mindfulness is also responsible for increasing telomerase, which is believed to help in the decrease of cell damage.

Mindfulness meditation has been shown to increase the production of antibodies that combat the flu virus. This shows that meditation can help boost our immune system.

WHAT MINDFULNESS TRULY MEANS

Mindfulness means being aware of the things happening right this very moment in both our immediate surroundings and in ourselves — our thoughts, our emotions, our physical sensations, and our behaviors. The purpose of this awareness is to prevent us from being controlled by these events. This awareness must be nonjudgmental and passing, that is, we focus only on the facts and accept them, avoiding our own evaluations or opinions, and then we let them go.

Suppose your boss has severely criticized you about the work you've done. You know that you do not deserve it – both the criticism and the way it was delivered, and so you become very angry.

However, instead of letting your emotions dictate your response, you take a step back and mindfully think about the situation. You say to yourself something like this, 'My boss is under a lot of pressure right now, cranky and easily angered. His criticism of me was unfair. I did not deserve it, and so I got furious.' And then you move on.

There are different psychotherapy skills associated with mindfulness, and the above example is only one application of them. Those who are learning these skills complete exercises, like meditation and mindful walking. But from this example alone, we can now easily understand and appreciate the benefits of mindfulness.

THREE STATES OF MIND

There is what is called the Wise Mind, which is one of the three states of our mind. This is the balance between our Reasonable Mind (when we act and behave based solely on facts and reason) and our Emotion Mind (when our thoughts and actions are dictated by our feelings). When we are using our Wise Mind — the wisdom in each one of us — we recognize and acknowledge our feelings, but we respond to them rationally.

The Wise Mind, or the practice of using our wisdom, is actually the first of the mindfulness skills. As illustrated in the example above, mindfulness helps us manage and control ourselves, especially in sudden and emotionally-intense situations, where we are more likely to react with our Emotion Mind. This benefit alone has many positive consequences in the long run — better relationships, more self-esteem and self-respect, better responses to unexpected crises, and lesser symptoms of anxiety and depression.

More importantly, when we are mindful, we also get to experience life more fully.

Mindfulness skills also train our minds, so we get the added benefits of improved memory, sharper focus, and faster mental processing. Our anxiety is also reduced, and we gain more control over our thoughts.

THE CORE MINDFULNESS SKILLS

And so, what exactly are these mindfulness skills? They are divided into three groups: Wise Mind, the "what" skills, and the "how" skills.

Wise Mind

As explained above, this is the middle state between our Reasonable Mind and Emotion Mind, where we recognize both our reason and emotions, and act accordingly.

The "What" Skills

These skills are in answer to the question, "What are the things you must do to practice mindfulness?" The answers are (1) observe, (2) describe, and (3) participate.

Observe

To observe is nothing more than to experience and be aware of our surroundings, our thoughts, our feelings, and the sensations we're receiving. This is stepping back and looking at ourselves, especially for reorientation when we are too preoccupied with our problems.

Describe

To describe is to put words to our present experiences — acknowledging what we feel, think, or do — and using only the facts to do it, without our own opinions. For example, we say to ourselves, "My stomach feels hungry," or "I'm thinking about my mother." Doing this lessens distraction and helps our focus.

Participate

To participate is to give ourselves fully to what we are doing at the moment (eating, talking, or feeling satisfied). We forget ourselves in it, and we act spontaneously.

The "How" Skills

These skills, on the other hand, answer the question, "How are you going to practice mindfulness?" The answers are: (1) non-judgmentally, (2) one-mindfully, and (3) effectively.

Non-judgmentally. A non-judgmental stance sees only the facts without evaluating, and without personal opinion. We accept each moment as it is, including our circumstances and what we see in ourselves: our thoughts, our feelings, our values, etc.

One-mindfully. Practicing mindfulness one-mindfully is doing only one thing at a time, and giving it all of our attention — whether that be dancing, walking, sitting, talking, thinking. This is about maintaining our focus and increasing our concentration.

Effectively. Practicing mindfulness effectively is keeping our goals in mind, and doing what is needed to accomplish them. We do our best, and we do not let our emotions get in the way.

These core mindfulness skills are central to Dialectical Behavior Therapy, and they support all the other skills. They are called "core" mindfulness skills because there are a few other skills or perspectives on mindfulness that are less commonly practiced. We will not talk about them in detail, but among these other perspectives is one taken from a spiritual point of view, designed for those who need further help in mindfulness in light of their spirituality.

MINDFULNESS EXERCISES

Now that we know the skills, it is time to apply them to exercises so that we can see them in action. The following is a small sample from the wealth of mindfulness exercises that have already been developed for DBT.

Meditation

To observe the present moment — in a nonjudgmental way — is the purpose of meditation.

To practice meditation, find a quiet place where you won't be disturbed. The goal is daily meditation of at least 30 minutes. For beginners, 10 minutes is advised.

Sit on a chair or a cushion on the floor. Sit with your back comfortably straight, with your arms at your side, and your palms on top of your thighs.

Then bring your attention to your breathing — pay close attention to your inhalation, exhalation, and the sounds they make. Try to do this for the entire duration. Your breathing is what you are using to ground yourself in the present moment.

However, your mind will soon wander, and that is all right. Simply acknowledge your thoughts without judgment, and then return your attention to your breathing.

You may also experience some uneasy feelings while meditating, and that is all right too. Again, simply acknowledge your feelings without judgment, and then return your attention to your breathing.

Do this again and again, always returning to your breathing whenever you are distracted, until the time is up.

Mindful Walking

Mindful walking is simply practicing mindfulness while walking, to observe one's own physical body and surroundings.

First, take note of how your body moves and how it feels as you take your steps. Notice the pressure on your feet, and the aches in your joints if there are any. Notice the increased rate of your heartbeat.

Then, expand your awareness to what is around you. What do you see? What do you hear? What do you smell? Do you feel the wind or the heat of the sun on your skin?

Five Senses

This is about using your five senses to observe your present moment. Notice at least one thing that you see, feel, hear, smell, or taste.

Mindful Breathing

You can do this mindfulness exercise sitting down or standing. If the time and place allow you to sit in a lotus position, do it, if not, no problem. You just need to ensure that you are focused on your breathing for at least 60 seconds.

Begin by slowly breathing in and breathing out. One cycle of breathing must last for about six seconds.

Remember to inhale through your nose and exhale through your mouth. Allow your breathing to flow without any struggle.

While doing this exercise, make sure that you can let go of your thoughts. Also, learn to let go of the things that you have to complete today or pending projects that require your attention. Let your thoughts flow their own way and focus on your breathing.

Be aware of your breathing, concentrating on your consciousness as air enters your body and gives you life.

Mindful Listening

This mindfulness exercise is intended to develop our hearing in a non-judgmental manner. This is also effective in training our brain to be less distracted by preconceptions and previous experiences.

The majority of what we feel is affected by our previous experiences. For instance, we may hate a specific song because it triggers bad memories of a moment in your life when you felt really bad.

Mindful listening is designed to allow you to listen to neutral sounds and music, with a present consciousness that is not blocked by any preconceptions.

Choose music or a soundtrack that you are not really familiar with. Perhaps you have something in your playlist that you have never listened to, or you may choose to turn on the radio to find music that you can listen to.

Close your eyes and plug in your earphones.

The objective is to suspend your judgment of any music you hear – its genre, artist, and title. Don't prejudge the label and try to go with the flow of the music.

Let yourself discover the music, despite the fact that you may not like it at first. Let go of your judgment and allow your consciousness to be with the sound.

Navigate the sound waves by discerning the vibe of every instrument used in the music. Try to separate every sound in your mind and assess each.

Also, be aware of the vocals – their tone and range. If the music has several voices, try to separate them as you did with the musical instruments.

The goal here is to listen mindfully, to become completely entwined with the music without any judgment or preconception of the music, genre, or artist. This exercise requires you to listen and not to think.

Mindful Observation

This mindfulness exercise is one of the easiest to do but is also among the most powerful because it allows you to appreciate the simpler aspects of your surroundings.

This exercise is intended to reconnect us with the beauty of our environment; something we often ignore when we are driving to work or even walking in the park.

- Select a natural object that you can easily focus on for a couple of minutes. This could be the moon, the clouds, an insect, or a tree.
- Try not to do anything except observe the thing you have chosen to focus on. Just relax and try to focus on the object as much as your mind allows.
- Look at the object and try to observe its visual aspects. Let your consciousness be consumed by the presence of the object.
- Let yourself be connected with the object's purpose and energy within the natural environment.

Mindful Awareness

This mindfulness exercise is intended to develop our elevated consciousness and appreciation of simple everyday tasks, as well as the outcomes they achieve. Consider something that you do every day that you usually take for granted, such as brushing your teeth.

When you grab your toothbrush, stop for a few moments and be mindful of your presence, your feelings in that moment, and what that action is doing for you.

Likewise, when you open the door before you go out and face the world, take a few moments to be still, and appreciate the design of your gateway to the rest of the world.

These things don't necessarily have to be physical. For instance, every time you feel sadness, you may opt to take a few moments to stop, identify the thought as harmful, accept the fact that human beings get sad, and then move forward, letting go of the negativity.

It can even be something very little, like every time you see a flower on your way to work, take a moment to stop and appreciate how fortunate you are to behold such a visual delight.

Select a touchpoint that really resonates with you today and rather than going through your everyday tasks like a robot, take a few moments to step back and develop purposeful consciousness of what you are currently doing, as well as the gifts these actions will generate in your life.

Mindful Appreciation

In this mindfulness exercise, you will be observing five things in your day that you often ignore. These things could be people, events, or objects. This is really your call. At the end of the day, write down a list of five things that you noticed throughout the day.

The goal of this exercise is to basically show your gratitude and appreciation of the things that may seem insignificant in life. That is, the things that also play their role in our human existence, but we often ignore because we focus way too much on the "bigger and more important" things in life.

There are so many of these little things that we barely notice. There's the clean water that nourishes your body, the cab driver who takes you to your workplace, your computer that allows you to be productive, your tongue that allows you to savor that delicious lunch you had.

However, have you ever taken just a few moments to pause and think about your connection to these things and how they play a role in your life?

- Have you ever stepped back and observed their more intricate, finer details?
- Have you ever wondered what your life would be like if these things were not present?
- Have you ever properly appreciated how these things give you advantages in your life and help the people you care about?
- Do you really know how these things really work or how they came into existence?

After identifying these five things, try to understand everything you can about their purpose and creation. That's how you can genuinely appreciate the way that they are supporting your life.

Mindful Immersion

Mindful immersion is an exercise that will help you develop satisfaction in the present moment and let go of persistent worry about what the future may bring.

Instead of anxiously wanting to complete our daily work so we can get on to the next item on the list, we can take the task and completely experience it. For instance, if you need to wash the dishes, focus on the specific details of the activity. Instead of treating this as a common household chore, you can choose to develop a completely new experience by taking a closer look at each aspect of your action.

Feel the rush of water when washing the plates. Is it cold water? Is it warm water? How does the running water feel on your hands as you do the dishes? Be aware of the movement you use in scrubbing off grease.

The concept is to be creative and find new experiences for a task that is quite monotonous and very common. Rather than struggling through and persistently thinking about completing the task, be conscious of each step, and completely immerse yourself in the process. Choose to take the task beyond a routine by aligning yourself with it mentally and physically – and even spiritually, if you're the spiritual kind.

MINDFULNESS IS FOR ANYONE

You have now learned what mindfulness is, its benefits, the skills associated with it, and the exercises to boost yours. You will need it not just in CBT but also in DBT and ACT, as you'll see in the following chapters.

Without a doubt, becoming more mindful and learning these skills are very useful and rewarding. It is not just a treatment option for those who are afflicted with a mental disorder. Learning to act wisely, despite our irrational feelings, and being more observant of ourselves and the things around us, is sure to bring us more happiness and contentment. Nurturing our ability to be aware of every moment in our life is a beneficial practice that can help us better manage the negative feelings and thoughts that may cause us anxiety and stress.

Through regular practice of mindfulness exercises, you will be far less likely to succumb to bad habits and become influenced by fear of the future and the negative experiences of your past. You can finally develop your ability to set your mind in the present and manage the challenges of life in an assertive yet calm manner.

You can, in turn, reshape your brain to harness a completely conscious mindset that is free from the bondage of self-limiting thinking patterns. This will allow you to be totally present to focus on positive emotions that could enhance your compassion, and finally understand yourself and the people around you.

CHAPTER 4: FUNDAMENTAL DBT SKILLS

DBT DISTRESS TOLERANCE SKILLS

The distress tolerance skills module of DBT acknowledges the higher tendencies in certain individuals to exhibit negative behaviors. It recognizes that, for such people, these behaviors may be overwhelming; therefore, they need to be addressed at once. It is common for such people to become overwhelmed even when the slightest amount of stress arises, and they often end up developing negative behaviors. To help these people, most conventional treatment approaches emphasize avoiding painful situations. However, in the distress intolerance module, the aim is to make the clients acknowledge that sometimes it is impossible to avoid pain, and the best way to tackle such situations is to accept the things as they are and practice tolerating the pain associated with them.

The concept of radical acceptance forms the foundation of the distress tolerance module. This means succumbing to the reality of a stressful moment and acknowledging that there is nothing you can do to change it. By practicing the concept of radical acceptance without fighting reality or being judgmental, patients become less vulnerable to developing prolonged and intense negative feelings.

The distress tolerance module in DBT comprises four different skills. These skills are meant to help individuals cope with difficult situations and experience distress without making it worse.

- Distracting
- Self-soothing
- Improving the moment
- Focusing on the pros and cons

Distracting

Distraction helps the patient shift their focus from upsetting emotions and thoughts to neutral or more enjoyable activities. It basically deals in anything to help distract you from the distress, for example, a hobby, a quick walk in the garden, helping others, or watching a movie. These activities help clients separate themselves from a distressing situation or a troubled state of mind.

The acronym "ACCEPTS" is used to help individuals practice the skill of distraction.

- Activities – Using positive activities to get over a distressing situation.
- Contribute – Helping out people around you or your community.

- Comparisons – Comparing yourself to people who have more difficult lives than you or to yourself at your worst.

- Emotions – Making yourself feel different by provoking a sense of happiness or humor with corresponding activities.

- Push away – Pushing your situation to the back of your mind for some time and replacing it with something less stressful on a temporary basis.

- Thoughts – Trying to forget what's distressing you and diverting your mind to think about other stuff.

- Sensations – Doing something intense to give yourself a feeling, which is different from the one that you are already going through, for example, eating a spicy meal or hopping into a cold bath.

Self-Soothing

The self-soothing module is all about teaching you to respect yourself and treat yourself kindly. It includes doing anything that helps you develop a positive image of yourself with the help of your 5 senses. For example, observing a beautiful view from the window (vision), enjoying the sounds of nature like birds chirping (hearing), lighting a scented candle (smell), enjoying a hearty meal (taste), and petting an animal (touch).

This skill entails using self-managed tools to calm clients when they are irritable and stressed. Learning to self-soothe is a significant milestone in the distress tolerance module of DBT. When you self-soothe, you treat yourself with care, kindness, and compassion. This helps you build resilience and makes it easier to bounce back from difficult situations.

Improving the Moment

In this skill, the basic aim is to utilize positive mental forces to improve your current image in your own eyes. This skill can be practiced by keeping in mind the acronym IMPROVE.

- Imagery – This includes visualizing anything that relaxes you in order to melt away the negative thoughts.

- Meaning – This includes deriving meaning or purpose from pain or a difficult situation. In simple words, it is all about finding a silver lining in everything you do. This helps the client find positivity in every situation and helps them learn something.

- Prayer – This includes praying to God to gain strength and confidence. Prayer tends to strengthen the spiritual side of many clients and helps them pacify themselves.

- Relaxation – This includes calming down your physical body and tensed muscles by doing relaxing activities such as listening to music, drinking warm milk, or getting a massage.

- One thing in the moment – This encourages the individual to be mindful and focus on a neutral activity going on in the present.

- Vacation – This includes encouraging clients to take a mental break from a difficult situation by imagining something pleasant or doing something that makes them happy. It can be anything, including taking a trip or simply ignoring all phone calls for some time.

- Encouragement – This involves making conversation with yourself in a supportive and positive manner to get through a tough moment.

The IMPROVE skill helps clients tolerate frustration or distress without making it worse, and in ideal conditions, aims to improve it. It is particularly for people who feel stuck in situations which are hopeless and out of their control. Such people are unable to do anything about these critical situations and hence, feel hopeless, hurt, and depressed. For many people, such a situation may feel like a constant crisis, so the use of the IMPROVE skill helps them get through this situation and regain confidence.

Focusing on Pros and Cons

With this particular skill, you are usually asked to make a list of all the pros of tolerating a stressful event and compare it with the cons not tolerating it (i.e. coping with it through self-destructive behaviors). The main idea of this is to help them remember how avoiding confrontation in a difficult situation in the past affected them in a negative way and to make them realize how it will feel to be able to tolerate the current stress without acquiring negative behaviors. This helps patients reduce impulsive reactions.

Summary

The distress tolerance skills taught as a part of DBT mainly focus on dealing with the suffering and pain that is inevitable to the human condition. The distress tolerance module provides the clients with beneficial tools to help them maintain their sense of balance in critical conditions. It teaches them to accept distress and manage it in healthier ways instead of acquiring negative behaviors. Following it supports the clients to learn how to authentically connect with other people, be open to your emotions, and respond flexibly to the ups and downs of life.

By practicing how to distract themselves, improve their current moments, self-soothe their mind and body, and balance the pros and cons of a particular situation, the clients are able to weather any distressing moment and reduce the destructive impulses and painful feelings. It will help them take a break and return to life in a calmer, rejuvenated, and more focused state, like a full gas tank which can now go on for miles.

DBT Interpersonal Effectiveness and Emotion Regulation Skills

We all go through millions of emotions on a daily basis. These emotions not only affect our own state of mind but also govern our interpersonal relationships which, in turn, define our personal and social lives. Dialectical Behavior Therapy acknowledges the importance of emotional regulation and interpersonal relationships and comprises two separate modules to address the problems related to these aspects.

DBT EMOTION REGULATION SKILLS

Emotion regulation forms an important module of Dialectical Behavior Therapy, with the purpose of teaching clients the necessary skills to get a hold of themselves in negative situations and focus on increasing positive experiences. Emotional regulation refers to a complex combination of ways through which a person can relate to and act on his/her emotional experiences. This generally includes understanding and accepting emotional experiences, the ability to rely on healthy strategies to manage uncomfortable emotions whenever necessary, and the skill of observing appropriate behaviors in a stressful state of mind.

"Control your emotions or be controlled by them."

It is common for clients with high emotional sensitivity to get stuck in a vicious cycle of negativity, often initiated by negative circumstances. These thoughts prompt an individual to respond by developing adverse or heightened emotions, eventually leading to harsh choices and self-destructive behaviors. More negative emotions, such as self-loathing or shame, may follow this detrimental behavior. For such clients, emotion regulation in DBT may be of significant help.

People who have good control of their emotion regulation are better able to control the urges to engage in impulsive behaviors like self-harm, physical aggression, or recklessness during times of emotional stress.

The DBT emotion regulation module comprises 3 goals:

1. To develop a better understanding of your emotions
2. To decrease emotional vulnerability
3. To reduce emotional suffering

A significant feature of DBT emotion regulation is making yourself understand that it is not bad to suffer from negative emotions. They are not something that you must struggle to avoid at all costs. You must make yourself realize that negative emotions are part of your normal life and will occur, no matter how hard you try to avoid them. At the same time, there are different ways of accepting these emotions and allowing yourself to better manage them so that you do not remain under their control.

1. Understanding Emotions and Naming Them

This skill involves recognizing emotions and labeling them. Clients are familiarized with the concept of descriptive labeling. They are then taught to use labels such as "anxious" or "frustrated" instead of general terms like "feeling bad." This is because vaguely defined emotions are much harder to manage. Another important aim of this skill is to teach the client the difference between primary and secondary emotions.

A primary emotion refers to your first response to any moment or triggers in the environment surrounding you. On the other hand, a secondary emotion refers to a response directed towards your own thoughts, for example, feeling sad about letting your anger out. These emotions are usually destructive and increase your likelihood of developing destructive behaviors. So, it is important to not only label your primary and secondary emotions but also to accept your primary emotion without judging yourself for having to deal with it in the first place.

In a normal DBT skill session, group leaders tend to discuss the myths relating to emotions that have plagued our society, for example, the common misinterpretation that there are certain "right" or "wrong" ways to feel in particular situations. An additional topic is to explain the primary purpose of emotions – which is to alert you that something around you is either problematic or beneficial. These emotional responses get stored in your memory and help you prepare yourself to encounter similar situations in the future. In addition to this, your emotions help communicate messages to others via words, body language, and facial expressions.

2. Decreasing Emotional Vulnerability

To practice this skill, a suitable acronym is PLEASE MASTER.

PL – indicates taking good care of your physical health and treating any illness or pain.

E – represents eating a nutritious and balanced diet and shunning foods with excessive caffeine, fat, and sugar.

A – indicates avoiding drugs and alcohol, which aggravate emotional instability and are not good for your mental health.

S – signifies getting adequate sleep on a daily basis.

E – involves exercising every single day.

MASTER – involves performing any task that builds competence and confidence every day.

This component of emotion regulation focuses on decreasing the emotional vulnerability by building positive experiences and balancing negative feelings. For this purpose, clients are asked to plan more experiences that bring them happiness and provide them with positivity. This may include participation in a sport or hobby, going out for coffee with a childhood friend, reading a good book, or doing any activity that provides them with individual contentment.

While doing these activities, clients are asked to remain mindful, focusing on what they are currently doing. If a client is finding it difficult to focus their attention on the current activity, they have a choice to try out another activity. Planning the future and establishing goals brings positive experiences for most clients. So, it is a part of this activity to plan ahead for the future, for example, choosing a different career or moving to a different city.

3. Reducing Emotional Suffering

Reduction of emotional suffering is the last part of DBT emotion regulation, which encompasses the following skills:

- Letting go
- Taking the opposite action

Letting go means using mindfulness to have complete awareness of your current emotional state. It further involves labeling this emotional state and allowing it intentionally instead of avoiding it, fighting it, or dwelling on it. This may require you to take a deep breath and imagine yourself floating away from the problem. Compare your emotion with a wave of water that keeps on coming and going.

Taking the opposite action includes engaging in certain behaviors that are opposite to whatever a person is feeling in the moment. For instance, if a person is sad, they may try to be active, stand straight, and speak confidently, as a person would if they were happy. When an individual experiences anger, they may behave as if they are calm by adopting a soft tone or doing something good for someone. This skill does not aim to deny the current emotion; the client must still name the emotion and be able to let it go. However, acting the opposite is likely to lessen the duration and intensity of the negative feelings.

DBT leaders try to make the clients learn these skills in group therapies. Sometimes, clients are asked to get involved in role plays to help them use these newly learned skills in their everyday lives. Ultimately, these skills help empower people to regulate their emotions instead of being regulated by them.

DBT INTERPERSONAL EFFECTIVENESS SKILLS

Interpersonal effectiveness means the ability to interact with other people. It encompasses all the skills you use to:

- Attend to your relationships
- Maintain a balance between priorities and demands
- Balance out your "wants" and "shoulds"
- Develop a sense of self-respect and mastery

The Importance of Interpersonal Effectiveness Skills

DBT considers interpersonal skills as important parts of the treatment because they teach us methods of communicating with other people. The way we communicate with others determines the quality of our social life which has a major influence on our overall well-being, self-confidence, and self-esteem. For this reason, interpersonal effectiveness is the main focus of DBT. In fact, it is taught as the second core skill module in DBT sessions, with lots of resources and materials dedicated to improving the interpersonal skills of the clients.

To enable the clients to establish communication with others, they are taught certain skills that help them get involved in everyday chats more thoughtfully and in a deliberate manner instead of speaking impulsively due to sheer stress or a distressing emotion. While there are a lot of skills associated with communication and interactions, DBT focuses on two components:

1. The skill of asking for things that you need or want

2. The skill to deny requests when suitable

DBT founder, Dr. Marsha Linehan, has identified three different forms of effectiveness that need to be addressed in this module:

- Objective effectiveness
- Relationship effectiveness
- Self-respect effectiveness

Under any circumstances, all the above-mentioned types must be taken into account. It is also important to prioritize them according to need, as this satisfies a person with their interactions as well as the outcomes.

'Objective effectiveness' refers to the goal or main motive behind a certain interaction that is directly linked to a tangible result. A typical example is a woman who wishes her husband would call her to inform her whenever he is working late. 'Relationship effectiveness' indicates the ultimate goal of a conflict-free relationship. In the previous example, the wife may rank harmony and emotional closeness as her first and highest priority. 'Self-respect effectiveness' can also be considered a priority in the case of this woman, if she starts feeling that her husband is being disrespectful by not calling her according to her wishes.

Dialectical Behavior Therapy utilizes different acronyms to help clients learn the skills tied to each type of effectiveness. In the case of objective effectiveness, DEAR MAN is the acronym of choice.

Describe: Describing the situation in solid terms, while avoiding any judgment.

Express: Expressing feelings and communicating them to the other party to let them know how the situation is making you feel.

Assert: Asserting your wishes and clearly stating what you want or do not want.

Reinforce: Reinforcing why you desire a particular outcome and rewarding people who respond positively to your request.

Mindful: Being mindful and investing your attention in the current moment, focusing on the task at hand.

Appear: Appearing confident, acquiring a confident tone and posture, and maintaining eye contact during conversations.

Negotiate: Being ready to get into negotiations, believing in "give and get," and acknowledging that everyone involved in the negotiations possesses valid feelings and needs.

For relationship effectiveness, the acronym used in DBT is GIVE:

Gentle: Approaching the other person in a non-threatening and gentle manner, avoiding judgmental comments and attacks.

Interested: Acting interested by giving others a chance to speak and listening to them wholeheartedly, and avoiding interrupting them just to give your own opinions or judgments.

Validate: Validating and acknowledging the wishes, opinions, and feelings of other people.

Easy: Assuming an easy manner by adopting a light-hearted tone and always having a smile on your face.

Lastly, the acronym used for self-respect effectiveness in DBT interpersonal effectiveness module is FAST:

Fair: Being fair to yourself and others to avoid the development of resentful emotions on both sides.

Apologize: Apologizing less and taking responsibility only when it is appropriate.

Stick: Sticking to your core values and not compromising your veracity in order to achieve a certain outcome.

Truthful: Being truthful while avoiding exaggeration or the portrayal of helplessness to manipulate others.

CHAPTER 5: LEARN NOT TO BE OVERWHELMED BY PAINFUL SITUATIONS

MANAGING STRESS USING DBT

The Distress Tolerance Skills taught as part of DBT can enable you to survive stressful situations without harming yourself. They may not provide you with strategies to help you in the long run but can help you learn skills to manage yourself successfully when times get tough. Strategies you can apply to get through intense stress include:

Distraction

Stress can cause you to get stuck in rumination and worry. Indulging your mind and body in a task that diverts your attention and prevents you from thinking about whatever is stressing you, at least for some time, can provide you with enough time to think about the stressor and ponder over how to get through it. Call a friend, work out, read your favorite book, or watch a funny movie to distract your mind from the stress.

Self-Soothe

Remember to be gentle and kind to yourself. It is common to be hard on yourself, especially during times of stress. You judge your abilities and feel like you are unable to handle your problems. Incorporating soothing activities in your everyday life can help you handle times of stress and tension. Listen to soothing music, bake cookies, watch a beautiful sunset, or eat your favorite food to soothe your body.

Try Relaxing

Following the distress tolerance module requires you to practice relaxation, for both the mind and the body. Try all the activities that will calm you. Take part in relaxation exercises or have a hot shower. Avoid performing multiple tasks at the same time, and try focusing on the current activity only. Form a soothing image in your mind.

Ponder the Pros and Cons

Take a paper and pen and make two lists stating the advantages as well as the disadvantages of a stressful situation. Pen down how stress can damage you if you do not care about it. Think of all the ways in which stress will help you evolve and grow as a person. Once you are done, go through the lists once again to motivate yourself.

Breathe

Observe your breathing pattern a little more closely. Try deep breathing or count your breaths to increase the focus of your mind. This can help you calm down and be more attentive.

Summary

These days, it is quite easy to fall into a rabbit hole and lose sight of the most important things in your life, all thanks to consistent stress. Keep in mind that in any moment of distress, you have control, even if this means letting go of things over which you have no influence. It may not be possible for you to solve every single problem in your life, but with DBT distress tolerance skills, you can definitely manage your frustrations much more confidently.

Do not let stress get the best of you!

MANAGING WORRY USING DBT

There is no overnight solution to managing worry, but there is one that actually works: DBT. The troubling thoughts might linger for a very long time, but you can easily develop a Teflon mind. It only requires a bit of effort.

Look for the Canaries in the Coal Mine

Recognize that the thoughts that are worrying you are nothing but thoughts. It may take time to develop this skill, but it is possible to adopt it relatively quickly. It is the negative emotions that are trickier to handle. These two may gang up on you; thoughts that are negative leading to emotions that are negative and vice versa; trapping you in an awful loop.

When you lose yourself in worrying thoughts, you have a tendency to forget your body. Try to recognize the physical sensations that follow your emotions such as sweating, shallow breaths and muscle tightening.

Get a paper and a pen and start making a list. Recall every little thought that crosses your mind when you are worried. Note down any physical manifestation that comes by during a stressful event. This is what you call finding the canaries in the coal mine. Notice what actions you take when you are worried (such as procrastination, drinking alcohol, etc.). Familiarize yourself with these actions, so that the next time worry strikes, you know what you are dealing with.

Avoid Avoiding

Why should you avoid avoiding? Because you should prove your worries wrong. If you keep avoiding triggers, it is just going to keep the anxieties alive in you. Worrying and then realizing that your concern was silly produces a phenomenon called "extinction," and the worry eventually stops.

On the other hand, persistently avoiding what you feel makes you believe these things are real and that fearing them is the right thing to do. This is what you call "reinforcement" and it only strengthens the worry.

Whenever your mind signals you to avoid a certain situation, recall that this is wrong. Allow yourself to appreciate the moment by considering it a chance to fight your fear and get away from your worries. Move your focus from the disturbing thoughts to the real world.

Now you know about the most important thing to avoid, let's move on to the one that you should be doing.

Identify

Do you at times look back at a moment of worry and think, "wow that really freaked me out?"

This is because you failed to realize this at the moment it occurred. Worries tend to sneak up on a person, and as you undergo cognitive fusion, the worries overtake you. This urges you to go and make bad decisions. The best way to bypass this problem and all the fuss it creates is by identifying the increasing anxiety before it is too late.

By now, you will have made your own canaries list. Great. Now what you should do is begin identifying these things as soon as they happen. The sooner you identify these thoughts, the action impulses, and the accompanying physical manifestations, the quicker you will be able to quell them.

It is easy to identify your problem once you understand what you are looking for. This enables you to control it or handle it, at least.

Engage

Have you ever found yourself swamped by troubling thoughts about a certain problem and a bigger trouble strikes you? This newly emerged problem forces you to forget about your past tensions and use whatever energy you have left in worrying about it. Notice how you are able to shift your attention. Doing it on purpose is, however, the tricky part.

The aim of this skill is to help you develop a connection with your feelings and experiences. It will help you learn how to remain in the current moment and establish a better connection with your life instead of wasting your energy on troubling thoughts. So, whenever you get stuck in a stressful or worrying situation, remember to focus only on the problem at hand while avoiding any worrying thoughts which may distract you.

Channel all your attention to living the current experience. If the worry is making you distracted, remember this point, and think only about the actual problem and make efforts to deal with it only.

Tend to Your Emotions

The first thing to do to tend to your emotions is to learn how to identify worry. Once you have recognized that you are stuck in troubling circumstances, observe your body closely. Look for any signs related to your heightened emotions. You may notice your heart pounding, your muscles tensing up, or your stomach sinking. Whatever you feel, pay close attention to it.

It is possible for your mind to divert its attention to any other topic. You may also feel like drowning in the pool of worries, which diverts your attention far from the actual problem. As soon as you find yourself in this situation, get yourself together. Try diverting all of your attention back to the body and focusing on the actual problem. Do not get involved in thoughts which are troublesome. You only need to notice them and keep returning your mind back to the body over and over again. Label your emotions, whether they are fear, anxiety, irritation, sadness, or shame. Remind yourself it is normal to feel how you are feeling right now, and your emotions are not going to kill you.

In short, examine, admit, and mark. The worrisome feelings will eventually dissipate. It is a skill, and it takes some time. But it definitely works. When you get good at it, it will be your superpower against worry.

Use Opposite Action

This may seem like advanced Kung Fu, so take it slow. In the end, this skill is what's going to take you from being a chronically worried individual to being a person who seldom worries. It is a mild form of "exposure therapy" and revolves around the concept of "facing your fears."

Opposite action helps your brain figure out which people and places are not dangerous, hence, do not need to be avoided. Once your brain is able to establish this connection, your fears start diminishing. You stop avoiding people or things and gain the freedom in life to do whatever you want and go wherever you like.

Take a moment to answer the following questions:

- Do you worry about things that do not pose a real or immediate threat?
- Do you worry so much that it becomes difficult to enjoy things?
- Are you more likely to be unhappy than happy?
- Are you unwilling to take reasonable risks?
- Does worry interfere with your day-to-day activities?

If you answer no to the questions above, you are likely a healthy person. So, keep doing whatever you are doing because you are only sensitive to real threats. You will take every reasonable step to live a happy life.

However, if the answer to most of the above questions is no, you are suffering from worry. It is necessary to take the steps mentioned above to take the unnecessary burden off your shoulders and start living.

Unfortunately, there is no magic pill that is going to relieve you or your worries overnight. Following DBT in a stepwise approach, as mentioned above can, however, significantly impact your life and make it easier for you.

DEALING WITH POST-TRAUMATIC STRESS SYMPTOMS USING DBT

DBT is a powerful method of thought control, which teaches you the necessary skills to deal with unpleasant thoughts and situations that lead to suffering. Through acceptance and change strategies, people suffering from PTSD can learn how to:

- Keep themselves aware of the triggers that cause negative reactivity
- Practice self-soothing activities to calm their body and soul
- Learn intolerance skills to deal with uncomforting feelings, situations, and thoughts

The DBT distress tolerance acronym ACCEPTS can help you manage PTSD. This skill stands for Activities, Contributing, Comparisons, Emotions, Push away, Thoughts, and Sensations. These techniques have been specially designed to manage your emotions and get over your past.

Activities

Engage in an activity. This can be any activity as long as it is healthy. Read a book, go for a walk, make some jam, or do the dishes. Anything that keeps you busy and your mind off the negative emotions associated with the past will help. When you are done, pick up a new activity. In this way, you can have a highly productive day without bringing back any haunting memories of the past.

Contributing

Do something kind for another person. Offering help can relieve you of your emotional stress in a lot of ways. An act of service is also a type of activity which will keep you distracted and take your mind off the problem. In addition to this, contributing will help you feel good about yourself. You are not always required to do something big. Help someone cook dinner, bake cookies for a relative, or offer to mow your neighbor's lawn. Each of these activities will keep you from remembering your misery.

Comparisons

It is time to put your life in perspective. Was there ever a time when you faced more difficult challenges than you are facing now? Maybe not. Maybe this is actually the most intense situation and emotion that you have ever experienced. In this case, compare yourself to another person. Has that person suffered more than you? Are you at home, comfortably lying in your bed after having a delicious dinner while in another part of the world someone is searching for leftover food in the trash and a place to sleep after suffering a natural disaster?

The purpose of this exercise is not to increase distress or the emotional pain of your current condition. Instead, use it to add a new perspective to what you are currently experiencing.

Emotions

You have the ability to invoke the opposite emotion of what you are feeling right now. Meditating for 15 minutes can help your anxiousness too. If a past trauma is making you depressed, watch a comedy movie. Adding a bit of the opposite emotion can help reduce the intensity of PTSD.

Push Away

If you feel like you are unable to deal with your past just yet, it is okay to push it away. Throw the problem out of your mind for a short duration. But how is this possible? By distracting yourself with other thoughts, activities, or mindfulness. You can set a time to come back and address your problems. Assure yourself that it will be addressed and stay calm in the interim.

Thoughts

Replace your anxious, negative thoughts with activities that occupy most of your mind, for example, reciting the alphabet backward or enjoying a Sudoku puzzle. These distractions will help prevent self-destructive behaviors and reliving the traumatic events until you achieve emotional stability.

Sensations

Make use of your five senses to soothe yourself during times of stress. A self-soothing activity can be anything such as taking a warm bath with relaxing music and a lavender bath bomb, eating your favorite food, or tuning in to a good TV show. Anything appealing to your senses can help you cope with PTSD for the time being.

These Dialectical Behavior Therapy skills can help you tolerate PTSD until you are able to resolve the problem once and for all. They can control the symptoms of PTSD and allow you to focus more on the present with no fragments of your traumatic past. While the ACCEPTS skills will enable you to focus on your current life, other modules of DBT, such as group therapy and interpersonal effectiveness, will motivate you to enjoy life at a basic level.

CHAPTER 6: EMOTIONAL CONTROL

Using Mastery

Using the mastery skills in this section will help you achieve Wise Mind. If you practice Wise Mind when the seas of life are calm, it will be easier to bring to mind those skills during times of turbulence.

Doing something that makes you feel a little better every day helps relieve stress and inspire confidence. Attaining confidence helps reduce stress in stressful situations as well as in everyday situations.

Taking care of yourself helps you stay grounded so that when difficulties arise, and they will, you can keep your cool and maintain a consistent level of emotions.

Build Positive Experiences

Building positive experiences is necessary for emotion regulation in that we need a well of positives to draw from when we're running on empty. Many experiences are wonderful at the time, and then we later may not be friends with the people we had the experience with. Do not let that mar the memory. Remember who they were when you had the experience together. There are two important categories in which to build positive experiences: the short term and the long term.

Short Term

Short-term memories include talking to a good friend, taking a walk, noticing a beautiful area, going to the dog park, reading a good book, watching a show or movie you love, dining out, having a picnic, and laughing on a break with a coworker. Most of us already do something to create short-term positive experiences daily without thinking about it.

This exercise asks you to create more short-term positive experiences and do it deliberately. Call up an old friend. Stay off social media after work for a few days. Make a concerted effort to tell ridiculous, silly stories with your kids. Send your nieces and nephews presents from the clearance aisle. Do something that will create positive experiences deliberately.

When you deliberately practice making and noticing positive experiences, you'll begin to make and notice more as part of your daily life. When positivity is a part of your daily life, you feel better emotionally and physically.

Do at least one of these things, or choose something else that makes you happy, every day for a week. Go out of your way to do it for a week. After that, try to make it IN your way. Do something you've never tried before. There are probably a few things you've never thought of trying:

- reading a good book
- writing a good story
- going out for drinks midweek

- going to a movie midweek

- sex

- eating a good meal

- going out just for dessert

- going to a poetry jam

- going to a karaoke bar

- joining pub trivia with friends

- learning to make sushi or another exotic dish

- trying a new exotic dish

- jogging

- kickboxing

- swimming

- watching a children's movie in the theater and focusing on the laughter

- stopping on the dog's walking route to smell the flowers

- doing something nice for a stranger

- doing something nice for a friend

- playing a carnival game

- getting the expensive, full inside and out car wash

- completing your to-do list

- writing a ridiculously easy to-do list so you can complete it

- taking pictures with a real camera

- going down a waterslide

- playing board games with friends

- playing interactive games, like "How to Host a Murder"

- going to a movie or concert in the park

- going to a new hobby class like painting or writing or learning to skate

- organizing your bookshelf or closet

- buying a new article of clothing, jewelry or book for yourself

- visiting a nursing home to sing or play bingo with the residents

- letting your kids teach you how to play their favorite video game

- getting a massage

- going to the chiropractor

- going to a play or the opera

- going to a high school play

- going to a college football game

- driving to a different city for dinner with a friend

- going sightseeing

- joining Toastmasters

- volunteering at a homeless shelter during the months they really need it: January-October

- carrying "homeless packs" in your cars: gallon Ziploc bags with personal hygiene materials, feminine hygiene products, smokes, granola bars, bottles of water, socks, candy bars, stuffed animals, cash, gift cards to McDonald's, etc. Put them with blankets, coats, and clothes you would've given away. Drive around the areas where there are homeless people and give these out.

- gardening

- planning a party

- getting your hair done

- talking in a different accent for an evening

- dedicating a song on the radio to someone

- writing in your journal

- spending some time alone without the television, radio, or internet; just you and a cup of the beverage of your choice

- going out to lunch with a friend
- playing volleyball
- playing hide and seek with your coworkers (and trying not to go home when their eyes are closed)
- singing in the car
- driving to the mountains
- roasting marshmallows
- going to the sauna
- sitting in a hot tub
- sitting in a cold tub
- making a fort in the elevator at work with a sign that says, 'No bosses allowed!'
- silently challenging the driver in the car next to you at a stoplight to a dance-off in your cars
- keeping a box of fruit snacks in your desk for anyone having a bad day
- having a song fight with your spouse
- convincing a stranger you think you're a vampire
- calling a radio station and telling them a funny story
- doing a jigsaw puzzle
- riding a unicycle
- going to a museum or aquarium
- going to a psychic, just for giggles
- getting a Reiki session done
- taking a stuffed animal for a walk, pretending to cry when anyone points out it's not real
- calling a radio station and pretending to be psychic. Google the DJ while you're talking and tell them all about themselves so they'll believe you.
- going to a belly dancing class

Long Term

Long-term positive experiences are more goal-oriented, creating a life worth living. What are some goals that you would like to achieve? Write down a few specific goals. Break them down into subcategories.

Money

- Many people have goals that are money-oriented. Write down how much you'd like to save each month or put towards your debt. If you put it in a place you'll forget or an IRA (Individual Retirement Account) you can't touch, you're less likely to spend it.

- Learn how to budget. Keep track of how much you spend versus how much you make. Keep track of all your expenses. See where you can cut back. Itemize your spending as you go – keep it on your phone until you put it into a spreadsheet. When tax time comes, you will already know how much you have spent on medical supplies or work-related expenses. Use your debit card instead of your credit card. Then you're only spending what you have, and if you don't keep your receipts, everything is on your bank statement anyway.

- Get out of debt as much as possible. You may always have debt for education, health, and home, but you can pay off your credit cards and chip away at the others.

- Save as much as possible. Save by packing your own lunch instead of eating out. Put that in a jar. Use those coins when your kid needs shoelaces or something. After a while of paying with change, you forget you ever had any dignity; it's cool.

- If your job offers a 401(k), take it. Immediately. The 401(k) follows the person, not the job. If your job offers overtime, do it. Pick up shifts. Show up in your uniform and ask who wants to go home. When a couple complains that they don't know where their waitress is, promise to take care of them yourself because she clearly doesn't value her customers. Then pocket that $20 tip. Find little tricks to make your job, and your screw-ups work FOR you.

Relationships

1. Repair a relationship.

If you have a relationship in your life that you feel must be repaired in order for you to move on with your life, you may have to take the initiative. You may have to make the first move, offer the first apology. Not a fake "I'm sorry you feel that way" apology, but a sincere "I'm sorry I treated you that way" apology. Not even a half-sincere apology – "I'm sorry I treated you that way, but you deserved it and here's why…" Let that second half come about if they accept your apology and you can open a discussion.

2. End a relationship.

Not all relationships can be saved, and not all should be. If you have offered a sincere apology and have been rebuffed, it may be time to cut your losses and move on. It may be sad for both of you, but some relationships over time become toxic for one or both parties. If this is the case, you might try one last-ditch effort, and then you should actually ditch it. If they come back, you can see how you feel at that time, and whether it's something you want to renew. Some relationships are better off dead. Reviving those is the true zombie apocalypse.

3. Create new relationships.

The older we get, the harder it is to create new relationships. We have to actually go out of our comfort zone to meet new people. Talk to people at your bowling league. Start a bowling league. Talk to new people at functions you attend regularly, like church or kayaking or suing people. Or even family reunions.

Go to weekly things. Join Toastmasters. You'll migrate towards the same people each week, but how much do you really talk to them? Get to know someone, more than at just surface level. Ask probing questions like, "If you invented a superpower, what would it be?" None of this already-invented superpower business. That's boring. "You can travel to the past, before a huge disaster, with the ability to warn people, but you might get stoned or burned as a witch, or you can travel twenty seconds into the future every day. Which do you choose?"

4. Work on current relationships.

Work on maintaining the relationships you have. Develop deeper bonds with people. Do you really know their hopes and fears, wishes, and dreams?

Go out of your way to stay in touch. Most friendships are built on convenience – when it's convenient for both or all parties to talk or hang out. Texting is a great way to let them know you're thinking about them, and they'll respond when they can. It's also a great way to miscommunicate, but that can be done in any medium.

Positive Mindfulness

1. Be mindful of positive experiences.

Practicing mindfulness while you're doing something you enjoy helps to savor the moment. Stay focused on the positive experience and refocus your mind as often as necessary. This will get you in the habit of mindfulness and focusing on the positive aspects of the day or the moment. The more we focus on something, the more we notice it. That's just how our brains work. That's not to say it is actually more prevalent, but it is certainly more prevalent in our minds, which is where we have to live, so we may as well learn to enjoy the company.

2. Be unmindful of worries.

Distract yourself from thinking you don't deserve this happiness, or wondering when the positive experience will end or thinking about what chores need to be done elsewhere. Distract yourself from thinking about what awaits you at the end of the positive experience, or worrying about how much money you're spending on it. If you're at the circus, for example, instead of thinking, 'I don't deserve to be enjoying this,' focus on your surroundings – children laughing, cotton candy, the rides, the clowns, unless you have a deep fear of clowns. You might not want to focus on them then. Damn you, Stephen King!

3. Practice.

There is a lot of material in this section, and no one expects you to conquer it overnight. You shouldn't either. Like any habit, it needs to be practiced before it becomes an actual habit. And then it still needs to be practiced.

Be Mindful of Positive Emotions

Get in the habit of noticing your emotions and recognizing whether they're negative or positive. When they're negative, get in the habit of not dwelling on them. When they're positive, get in the habit of being mindful of the actual emotion. "I'm happy right now. It feels warm. It feels calm." Describe how the emotion feels, instead of getting caught up in why you're happy or peaceful, or what have you.

Using the Opposite to Emotion Action

What actions do you do with negative emotions? They're probably the go-to actions, preprogrammed by your psyche. It takes time, but you can reprogram your psyche by using the opposite actions you normally use. When you're afraid, your brain kicks in to fight, flight, or freeze mode. In some instances, this is still a vital response mechanism developed for our own safety. In other instances, the response mode has been passed down from our hunter/gatherer ancestors and serves no real purpose today. For example, test anxiety. It's real.

A test doesn't present the need for a fight/flight/freeze response that imminent death, beating, rape, a car accident, or a full-grown saber-toothed tiger would pose. However, the reaction is still the same, and we don't get to choose our subconscious reactions. But we do choose our conscious actions. In the test anxiety example, try giving yourself many practice tests to lose your anxiety.

Perhaps your fear is roller coasters. Go more often, with someone you feel safe with to desensitize you. Try to desensitize yourself to the fear. If your fear is clowns, go to McDonald's more. No need to hang around real clowns. Those freaks will eat you in your sleep.

If your reaction to anger is to yell and throw things, step away from the situation that makes you angry and work on breathing exercises. Unless you're driving. Then just work on breathing exercises.

If a particular person or politician makes you angry, try to find the small amount of truth they may have said to gain sympathy or empathy, or at the very least, not hatred. Scratch that. Turn off the television. Work on that with a real person in your life rather than a politician.

If your go-to reaction to sadness is self-isolation, take the opposite approach. Get out in the community and volunteer. Go out with your friends. Go to an ice cream store by yourself, just to get out of the house. And have some ice cream.

If you're feeling shameful, the first question to ask yourself is, "Why am I feeling like this?" Is it because you did something you're ashamed of? Admit it to yourself and your haters, then move on. The longer you deny it, the longer it draws out the feeling and adds further negative emotions to it, like anger. If you've done nothing wrong, but are being dragged through the mud for pointing out something someone else did, welcome to the patriarchy. Even males can be oppressed by it. Just hold your head high and live your life. People will soon see who you really are. And those who don't see it often filter out. Let them.

Guilt works in many ways, as does shame. If you need to offer a sincere apology, do so. Your refusal to do so, whether it's accepted or not, whether they've offered one or not, whether they actually deserved whatever action you need to apologize for or not – that's all irrelevant. Your refusal to do so only drives the wedge in further.

The opposite reaction works best when the emotion does not fit the scenario. If you should be angry at something, it's still best to breathe deeply and assess the situation calmly. However, the other person is allowed to know you're angry. If your anger motivates you toward positive change, so much the better.

CHAPTER 7: INTERPERSONAL EFFECTIVENESS

Using Objectiveness Effectiveness (D.E.A.R. M.A.N.)

D – Describe

Describe the event using facts only. Do not use emotions. Let it speak like a police report if you do use emotions. "Patient seemed upset." It works better to sound like a police report if you talk in third person. However, don't take this habit into the real world. That's just confusing. Don't make a request or "dry beg." Dry begging is saying obnoxiously passive-aggressive things like, "I really need thirty bucks," or, "Wow, that cake looks good. I wish I had some." The best response to dry beggars is: "Yep. You do." Or it could be, "Yep. It is." If they really want it, they'll get around to asking like an adult. It might go like this – say you're from a religious family, and your teenager decides not to go to church. You might reply, "I've noticed you don't like church. Let's discuss the options of staying home."

This is important so that the other party understands clearly what the situation is before you ask anything, entreat, or make an executive decision.

E – Express

Express yourself with "I feel" or other "I" statements. These types of statements help the speaker take accountability and prevent the listener from immediately going into defense mode. Let's go back to the teenager staying home from church example. Now, you might say something like, "I feel like you should believe what I believe, but I know that you're your own person, separate from me, and I can't force my beliefs on you. I would like you to come to church with us because my worry is you won't be productive at home."

This is important so that the other party understands where you're coming from when you express how you feel about the situation you've just described.

A – Assert

Assert your position by either directly asking for what you need or stating your position clearly. Don't beat around the bush, don't use euphemisms, and don't hesitate to the point of losing the other party's interest. To continue with the example, let's assert our decision for our hypothetical teenager. "I understand that you don't want to come to church with us, and you are old enough to stay home alone. So, if you choose to stay home instead of attending church, you will prepare dinner and set the table and have everything prepared for us to be able to eat when we return, and you will make enough in case we invite people over unexpectedly. If you are unable to complete this chore, and thus, be productive for the whole family while we are at church, you will come back with us, even if you don't believe it."

This is important because ambiguity creates miscommunication in relationships, and that is the biggest source of contention. Be unambiguous. Set boundaries now. If you're making a request, it must also be unambiguous, maybe even a little lawyerly.

For example, you might say, "Can I please borrow your car from Sunday to Tuesday? I'll return it by 7:00 pm with a full tank of gas and a wash."

The other party might have other caveats. Such as, "Yeah, but it overheats, so don't go over 55 mph, or over 55 miles away. And my tags are expired, so avoid cops. Or renew it for me."

In which case, you might say, "You know what? I can take the bus. Thanks, though."

R – Reinforce

Make sure the other party knows why they should grant your request, or acquiesce to your conditions without a fight. "Because I said so" is not a valid reason. Most people reciprocate naturally.

You might say something like, "You get to stay home from church on the condition that you are productive at home. Since you don't like church and I don't like cooking after church, it's a win for both of us."

Or in the example with the car, it might sound like this, "I actually need to drive to a different city for a few days, but I can't rent a car because of (XYZ), so I'll get your car diagnosed for you, and if I can afford to fix the overheating problem, I will. If not, I'll see if anyone else can part with their car for a few days, or find another solution."

In both examples, the other party can clearly see that they have nothing to lose by accepting your request, and everything to gain.

This is important because relationships are built on reciprocity. When one party feels slighted occasionally, it's not a big deal. But if one party feels slighted more often than not, they will most likely end the relationship.

M – Mindful (stay)

Stay focused on the conversation. If you're answering a text, they have no reason to listen to you. If they're answering a text, that's out of your control, but you can keep your mind on the conversation instead of what they're doing. If they become defensive, notice what you may have said wrong, and apologize if necessary, even if it's just to get them back on track.

This is important because it's too easy to go off track and lose focus, especially in an uncomfortable situation, where the other party might be looking to pick a fight. If you go off on tangents, whether they be to sing and dance because someone said a song lyric, or to fight, or because one of you saw a squirrel, you have less of a chance of getting what you want. Especially if you're the one singing and dancing or chasing squirrels.

Your teen may interrupt you to tell you they've been cutting church every week with their friends from Sunday School anyway, so there's no point in going. You may have to repeat yourself a few times, especially if you're letting them stay home as long as they're productive, as they may not believe their ears.

Again, repeat yourself as often as necessary, and if you have a real kid, you've done that a few times already this morning. And bring the conversation back to the topic. Detour…focus. If we're using the example of asking an adult friend for something, you don't have the clout you do as a parent. You still may have to repeat yourself, but the interruptions might just be singing and dancing.

You might say something like, "I understand you don't like church, and you cut Sunday School anyway. But you will get something out of it every week if you continue going, and I would like that." Or, "If you're going to stay home, you'll need to cook for us, and I'll take the added precaution of changing the Wi-Fi password every Saturday to make sure you'll be productive. If you can prove that you are, that you don't have friends over, that you cook and clean as you go, I'll stop doing that."

A – Appear Confident

Appear confident no matter how you actually feel. If you have this look about you all the time, little old ladies will ask you for a napkin at a restaurant when you're on a date, and it might not even occur to you to tell them you don't work there, so you walk into the kitchen and get the napkins.

Your nonverbal cues indicate confidence more than your verbal cues. Sit with your back straight, and your head held high. Make eye contact. Orient your feet towards the other person. Where your feet are oriented is where your mind subconsciously goes. Appear confident and stand your ground.

This is important because confidence signifies that your request isn't too difficult to grant and that you're harder to turn down. There's no need to be overbearing. If they do refuse you, in an adult-to-adult conversation, you might just ask if they're sure, then thank them for their time and let it go.

If your teenager refuses you, this might be a good time to tell them what the other option is. "Okay, you don't have to learn to cook. And if you can read, you can cook, by the way. You can keep coming to church with us, and thank you for letting me know about cutting Sunday School. I'll be sure to tell your friends' parents you all do that because they'll want to know too. I'll let them know you told me. Thank you for caring about the salvation of your friends, who also should go back to church." This will most likely ensure you an excellent meal every Sunday.

N – Negotiate

Negotiate. Remember, "give to get," as selfish as that sounds. Everyone wonders,

What's in it for me? You aren't demanding something. You're asking for something or setting down a rule. Even in setting down rules, you aren't demanding. If you think you can demand something of someone, even a child, expect defensiveness and confrontation. Give options.

You may need to alter your request to make it more pleasing. In the borrowing the car example, you offered to get the car diagnosed (AutoZone does it for free) and fix it if you could – and if you couldn't, you'd find another solution to your problem.

This is important because building relationships may or may not be the most important reason we spend a few decades on this planet, but it certainly takes up most of our time. Whether we spend that time in actual relationships with other human beings or wondering why we drive other human beings away, we spend an inordinate amount of time either with other people or thinking about them, whether we know them personally or not.

So, if we spend our energy browbeating others and expecting them to kowtow to us, that only works if you have money, and even then, not everyone likes you, even if you somehow win elections. Mere mortals, without insane amounts of money, can't behave like that. We have to negotiate and play nice.

Going back to the example of the teenager, this is pretty much already a negotiation. They still refuse to go to church or cook, and they tell you they don't care if you call their friends' parents. They really do. This is when you pull out your phone and look up the numbers of the kids' parents, who you probably know, at least by name already. Google White Pages are great. Some rules are not to be negotiated. If, however, you start the conversation with trying to force them to go to church, this idea is a perfect negotiation, and now it seems (to them) that you've given in some.

But for example's sake, you do try to negotiate. You might say, "Okay, if you don't come to church with us on Sunday, you still need to be productive at home. Would you rather have a list of chores to do? What is your suggestion for being productive, other than homework, because I don't want you deliberately putting it off until Sunday?"

This approach helps your child feel like they have a say – like their voice is heard and not invalidated. If you start off demanding they go, then negotiate to this, you can offer it as a suggestion, and ask which of your suggestions they like best.

You can both leave the conversation feeling like you've accomplished something, like you've got a win, like you're helping the other person out, with no ill will.

INTERPERSONAL EFFECTIVENESS EXERCISES

Step 1 - Choose an area in your life that you want to work on.

This may include community, romance, education, career, personal growth, environment, family, parenting, health, finances, and many more.

Step 2 - Establish goals that are SMART - Specific, Meaningful, Adaptive, Realistic, and Time-Bound.

Specific - Try to be as specific as possible as to what actions you want to take. Be sure that you are aware of the involved steps in taking the necessary action. A specific goal is easier to achieve compared to a general goal. For example, just setting up the goal of spending more time with your child may not allow you to know if you have already achieved it. A more specific goal is to have at least a one-hour playtime every day. Being specific with your goal will allow you to assess whether you have already accomplished the goal or not and monitor your progress.

Meaningful - Assess if your goal is genuinely based on your values in comparison with a strict rule or a sense of what you must do. If you think that your goals don't have a deeper sense of purpose or meaning, try to assess if the goal is really influenced by the values you hold dear. Take note that your core values should be based on things that provide meaning to your life.

Adaptive - Make sure your goal will help you follow a direction that you think will greatly improve your life. Assess if your goal will move you closer or is steering you away from the real purpose of your life.

Realistic - There's a big chance that you will only feel disappointment, frustration, or failure if you set goals that are not really attainable. Try to find a balance between setting goals that are quite easy versus goals that are impossible to achieve. Be realistic and practical so you can really push yourself to achieve your goals.

Time-Bound - You can specify your goals even more by adding a time and date by which you want to accomplish them. If this is not possible, or not realistic, try setting up a time frame and doing everything you can to make certain that you work within this limit.

Step 3 - Define the Urgency of Your Goals

The last step is to define the urgency with which your goal should be accomplished. Your goals could be:

- Long-term - Create a plan of the necessary actions you need to take so you can be closer to your goals over the span of six months to one year.
- Medium-term - Think about the necessary actions you need to take so you can move towards your goals within two to three months.
- Short-term - Make a list of the things you need to do so you can achieve your goals within a month.
- Immediate - What are the goals that you need to achieve within a week or even within the day?

Starting to live in accordance with your personal core values will fan the flames of your committed action.

Our best plan and values will not be meaningful if they are not supported by action. Equipped with the knowledge of the core values you really want to pursue, you can start moving forward towards living a valuable life.

TIPS FOR A BETTER LIFE

What to avoid when trying to improve your self-esteem:

Putting other people down. Sometimes, when a person doesn't feel so great about themselves, they may have to resist the urge to tear someone else down. A great way of being masterful at this is to avoid comparing yourself to others. When you feel a sense of inferiority, then you may try to pull others down so you feel better about yourself. However, if you are not in competition with others then it's less likely that you'll feel inferior to them. When you put other people down, the positive feeling only lasts temporarily, and you don't get a positive response from others; in fact, it often just makes things worse. Focus on your own uniqueness, and not comparing yourself with others.

Thinking you're better than others. You are not better than anyone else, and no one else is better than you. This is a universal truth that all should embrace. When you start to tell yourself that you're better than other people, then you're essentially trying to replace your feelings of unworthiness with the unhelpful belief that other people are not as good as you. This tendency will ultimately make your relationships worse. Again, you should focus on your inherent value and uniqueness instead of trying to make yourself believe that you are above other people. Truly masterful people are so convinced of their own self-worth that they actually want to encourage others to have a masterful life too.

People pleasing. Often, people who are chronic people-pleasers also have a chronic and deeply-felt dislike of themselves, to the point that they feel like they have to win the approval of others. Often this dislike is subconscious, so you may not be aware of it. However, you do not have to be desperate for others to like you and approve of you. Whether they do or not does not change your own inherent value and self-worth.

Refusing constructive criticism. Everyone, without exception, has some areas that could benefit from some improvements. This is part of what makes you human. The consistent development of a person is a part of their ultimate destiny. No one ever totally arrives at it, as self-actualization is in the process. When you refuse constructive criticism, it signals that you believe critique means that you're inadequate. Change your beliefs to include the more helpful alternate belief that everyone needs healthy constructive criticism to become unstuck and continue to evolve as a person. Don't be ashamed of your shortcomings or try to use perfectionism to cover up weaknesses. Instead try to recognize them, receive constructive criticism, and grow in the process.

Avoiding failure or rejection. If you're constantly living life in a manner that you think will help you avoid failure or rejection, then you will probably benefit from revising your thoughts and creating some healthier alternatives. Temporary failure is inevitable at times and rejection may rear its ugly head periodically. However, you must learn how to tolerate the distress and keep moving forward or else you'll end up being stagnant out of fear of failure and rejection.

Avoiding emotions. Trying to block emotions is not healthy, nor is it something that is sustainable long-term. Having a wide range of emotions is a part of the human experience, and being strong doesn't mean avoiding them. Allow yourself to fully experience negative emotions and then use strategies to change the situation or change your thoughts about the situation.

Trying to control others. That is not your job. You do not have to prove your significance by trying to make other people conform to what you want. Instead, focus on your own self-improvement.

Over-defending your self-worth. No one is saying you have to be a doormat for others to stomp all over, but if you find you are compelled to always defend yourself, then that's an indicator that you're struggling with self-confidence. If you are okay with your own inherent self-worth, you won't feel the need to constantly defend yourself. Don't allow yourself to become outraged every time a person says something about you that you don't like or offers an opinion that differs from your own. Instead agree to disagree, tolerate any negative emotion, change how you think about your own inherent self-worth and keep moving forward with your goals. Remember, you can show yourself respect even if other people don't respect you in the same way.

Blaming other people for your problems. Of course, you have had your share of difficulties. In fact, more than half the American population has had some traumatic experience, so you are in good company. What separates people who accomplish their goals from people who don't are their attitudes and behaviors. Do not blame nature or other people for your problems. Don't blame your past, genetics, hormones, or anything else for what you're currently experiencing. Focus on accomplishing your goals and don't get sidetracked by playing the blame game.

Don't take yourself or life so seriously

Understand that you will make mistakes. You are human, which means that without question, you will make mistakes at some point in your life. During some stages of your life, you will make more mistakes than others. The key is to course-correct by changing your thinking and behavioral patterns. Expect that sometimes you will make mistakes and that they are important, because the lessons you learn are key for your own personal development.

Try new things. Don't be so afraid to try something different. The more you try new things, the more things you'll find that you're good at. Also, you'll become more confident as you see that trying new things can actually turn into positive experiences. If you "fail," surely you will have learned something in the process.

Be silly on purpose. This is a great way to avoid being ashamed when you mess up. Purposely engage in a silly activity in public. For instance, wear a big crazy hat on the train or walk through the mall wearing a loud, colorful, mismatched outfit. Practice self-acceptance skills while you're doing these silly things and you'll discover that you're not as easily shamed anymore.

Laugh at yourself. It really is that simple. When you feel the urge to be overly critical, or you start to feel shame creep up, begin to laugh at yourself. Stop taking yourself so seriously. Things happen. Learn to laugh about it instead of ruminating about it.

When in social situations, focus on things other than your own performance. Take the focus off of yourself and move your attention to a more external focus. What are your friends doing and saying? What does the atmosphere look like? What are the smells you're experiencing? Try to identify them. Enjoy the flavors of any meal you're enjoying. Try to be mindful of your environment instead of focusing on internal thoughts and impulses. This is a great distraction technique. Be intentional about not having a requirement to feel absolutely safe in your environment and learn to enjoy yourself.

Creativity. Tap into your creative side. If you have natural creative talents, express them. Take some time to participate in activities that you truly enjoy. The more masterful you become with your creative endeavors, the better and more confident you will feel overall.

Be adventurous. Stop trying to avoid unpredictable outcomes. The chances of you being able to accurately predict the outcome of every situation are slim, and your tendency to be overly cautious only makes life more chaotic for you.

CHAPTER 8: FREQUENTLY ASKED QUESTIONS

How are CBT and DBT different?

DBT has its roots in CBT, but it uses a more dialectical approach than traditional CBT therapies. Although most people are able to get significant results from CBT, it was found that there was a specific group of patients who were not getting the results that the average person was receiving. Instead, this group got frustrated with the process and quickly dropped out because they did not feel validated. So, a revised CBT process that combines emotional validation with behavioral change was developed. This is known as DBT.

Are CBT and DBT more effective than other therapies?

These therapies have been scientifically proven to be very effective, and most clients make lasting changes quickly. All therapies have their positive points however, cognitive-based therapies are often favorites among clinicians because they are action-oriented, thus obtaining in quicker results. The results that most people get in a year of talk therapy can be easily obtained in 3-4 sessions of CBT or DBT.

How does the therapy work?

The amount of therapy you need varies based upon your own individual needs, however most people do well with one individual session per week. DBT also includes one additional skill-building group session per week. Your commitment to the therapy process really is the best determining factor as to how the therapy will work. Some people do more than one individual session per week, while others are comfortable with the one session. That is something that you should discuss with your therapist to determine a specific treatment regimen.

How long does it take to see progress?

Progress varies depending on the person, but most people start seeing results very early, typically within 3-4 sessions. Of course, this depends largely on how much effort you put into the program. Doing the homework consistently and attending the group skill-building sessions every week is critical to your success in DBT. This book provides many of the techniques that you will learn during treatment.

What if I'm skeptical?

Give it a try. You won't know whether it works or not until you try it. Just like almost anything else in life, you won't know how effective it really is until you try it. Commit to doing your first behavioral experiment and see how it goes. If it works, great, keep going. If it doesn't, you can always stop.

Can I discontinue medication?

Although both CBT and DBT have both been found to be quite effective treatment approaches, even without medication, the decision to discontinue your medication should be taken very seriously and supervised by a medical professional. You should discuss that decision with your psychiatrist or another physician.

How does DBT prioritize treatment goals?

- Target 1: Life-threatening behavior and behavior that interferes with treatment
- Target 2: Decrease emotional suffering
- Target 3: Daily living management
- Target 4: Sense of wholeness and connectedness

This is the priority of the goals for DBT treatment. Of course, life-threatening goals take priority and moving through suicidal ideation or self-harm behavior is addressed first. Also, behavior that interferes with treatment is high-priority as well because no progress can be made unless there is commitment to the therapy process. The ultimate goal is to get you to a place of complete wholeness. You are one out of a whole universe, and you are universally connected with every other person in the universe. Whatever your religious or spiritual beliefs are, the ultimate goal of DBT is to help you embrace yourself, your life, and other people so that you can fully experience and enjoy life.

Is Eastern philosophy an underpinning of DBT?

DBT's core mindfulness component emphasizes staying in the present, and it does have its foundation in Eastern traditions. The goal is to help you stay in the present with your thoughts and emotions because most disturbances result from things that have happened in the past or thoughts about the future. The tradition of concentrating on the here and now has been practiced in the Eastern world for centuries and the Western world has more recently adopted the mindfulness theory. It has been very helpful for people who truly want to get unstuck so that they are no longer overwhelmed by their emotions.

CONCLUSION

Dialectical Behavior Therapy has offered much in the realm of therapies. Dr. Linehan has saved thousands of lives with her innovative work. Borderline Personality Disorder is not being "crazy" or "unhinged." It's simply mental illness. It includes many other mental illnesses as facets of it. Because of that, it only makes sense that an effective therapy for this condition would include many types of therapy and self-reflection.

Mindfulness is probably the most important aspect of DBT because we have been trained not to be mindful. We're like ants, scurrying around – hurry, hurry, hurry, but going nowhere.

Mindfulness forces you to focus on the present. Ask yourself, "Am I treading water? Am I at the bottom of a ladder I want to be on or the middle of one I don't?" When you choose mindfulness, you look at your life for a moment.

Your questions aren't all going to be answered in one moment of mindfulness. It's something that must be practiced every day. DBT is an excellent medium for learning the skills of mindfulness and interpersonal relationships. When therapy is complete, you've acquired an outstanding toolkit of skills to reach for in any situation.

Our entire lives are our memories and our interpersonal relationships. Because DBT focuses on mindfulness and interpersonal relationships, it is one of the most effective types of therapies. When we're mindful, we're creating memories. We're technically creating memories when we're not mindful as well – but not memories of what's actually happening.

In summary, by practicing the skills of DBT, we create memories and interpersonal relationships. And having good memories and relationships is what makes life worth living.

CPSIA information can be obtained
at www.ICGtesting.com
Printed in the USA
LVHW111103020122
707652LV00005B/324